all*you

Frightfully Fun

HALLOWEEN HANDBOOK

By Carole Nicksin and the editors of ALL YOU magazine

Contents

9

114

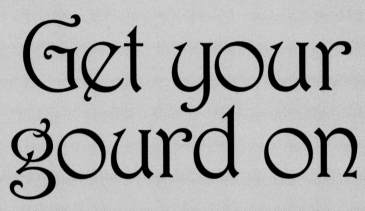

Get your gourd on

Get in the spirit by making a few pumpkin decorations for your front porch, your dining room table and anywhere else you want to inject some seasonal fun.

Make a face

...or try something less traditional, like a polka-dot or striped pattern. There's virtually no limit to the different ways you can dress up a plain old pumpkin, squash or gourd.

Button heads

℘☠℘

YOU'LL NEED ✦ **Hot-glue gun** ✦ **Assorted black buttons** ✦ **Pumpkins** ✦ **Black pipe cleaners** ✦ **Sharp pencil**

1 Glue buttons to pumpkin to create face, using a line of buttons for mouth.

2 Wrap pipe cleaners around sharp pencil to make corkscrew curls.

3 For "girl" pumpkins, poke holes around crown of pumpkin with sharp end of pencil and insert pipe cleaners; secure pipe cleaners with dabs of hot glue.

Masked banditos

℘☠℘

YOU'LL NEED (makes 1 masked pumpkin) ✦ **Scissors** ✦ **Bandit mask templates (page 164)** ✦ **Black felt** ✦ **White chalk** ✦ **Rickrack, gold-tone cord, rhinestones or glitter** ✦ **Craft glue** ✦ **1 yard black ribbon** ✦ **Pumpkin** ✦ **Googly eyes**

1 Cut out template—the regular size works for most pumpkins; the small size is for mini pumpkins approximately 3" in diameter.

2 Place template on black felt and use chalk to trace it, including eyeholes. Cut out mask and eyeholes.

3 Decorate mask with rickrack, gold-tone cord, rhinestones or glitter. Use craft glue to adhere.

4 Cut ribbon into two lengths. Attach a ribbon to each side of mask, gluing ends to inside corners (wrong side). Let dry.

5 Tie mask around pumpkin. When mask is in position, glue googly eyes on pumpkin.

WITCHY WOMAN
Cut 2 holes into gourd for eyes; push mini gourds into holes. Cut another hole on bottom and fit pumpkin stem into hole. Glue on raffia for hair. Shape a mouth and buttons from pipe cleaners and glue on. Place hat on top.

USE SMALL GOURDS AS TABLETOP DECORATIONS

Ghostly gourd

∽❧☠❧∾

YOU'LL NEED ✦ X-acto knife ✦ **Pointed-top gourd** ✦ **2 oblong pumpkins** ✦ **White spray paint** ✦ **Toothpicks** ✦ **Cheesecloth**

1 Carve a mouth and eyes into gourd. Hollow out and carve *boo* into one pumpkin.

2 Spray gourds and pumpkins white; let dry.

3 Assemble pieces to look like a snowman, using toothpicks to hold them in place. Drape stack with cheesecloth.

Screaming spirits

∽❧☠❧∾

YOU'LL NEED (makes 1) ✦ **Acrylic pearlescent white craft paint (at craft stores)** ✦ **Paintbrush** ✦ **Mini spoon gourd** ✦ **Plastic garbage bag** ✦ **Clear plastic bottle (any 12- or 16-oz. bottle will do), empty** ✦ **16-oz. bottle Aleene's fabric stiffener and draping liquid** ✦ **Large mixing bowl** ✦ **22" square of white fabric, such as from an old sheet** ✦ **Silver glitter, optional** ✦ **Black medium-point felt-tip pen** ✦ **Hot-glue gun**

1 Paint gourd and set aside to dry.

2 Place garbage bag on work surface and set empty plastic bottle in center.

3 Pour fabric stiffener into mixing bowl and add fabric, making sure it is completely saturated with stiffener.

4 To make ghost body, wring out fabric slightly and center over top of plastic bottle. Drape fabric and arrange folds until you create desired shape. Allow to dry overnight.

5 Optional: For extra sheen, once ghost body has dried completely, paint and sprinkle with glitter while paint is still wet. Let dry.

6 Use pen to draw a spooky face on painted gourd; secure gourd to top of ghost body with hot glue.

Scary skulls

꩜☠꩜

YOU'LL NEED (makes 1) ✦ **Serrated knife** ✦ **White pumpkin** ✦ **Large metal spoon** ✦ **Paper towels**
✦ **Washable marker** ✦ **All-purpose cleaner** ✦ **Tweezers**

1 Working carefully, use knife to cut around pumpkin stem. Remove lid; use spoon to scrape away pumpkin seeds and strings.

2 Dry pumpkin exterior with paper towel. Use marker to draw skeleton face on pumpkin. If you make a mistake, use paper towel and all-purpose cleaner to erase.

3 Once design is complete, cut out eye sockets and nostrils (if desired).

4 To create mouth, cut a wavy horizontal line (going across pumpkin ridges) below nostrils to desired length. Cut a parallel wavy line ⅛" below first line. Make small vertical cuts at each end of mouth to connect lines. Using tweezers, carefully remove thin pumpkin slice.

5 For the teeth, cut out slender triangular shapes above and below mouth opening, using tweezers to pull out pieces.

PAINT IT BLACK
If you have a bunch of
mismatched pots, plates
and bowls, spray-paint
them black to create a
unified display.

Steampunk totem pole

۞ ☠ ۞

YOU'LL NEED ✦ Scissors ✦ 2 pieces brown felt and 1 piece black felt ✦ Empty 6-oz. can tomato paste, cleaned ✦ White chalk ✦ Hot-glue gun ✦ Brim template (page 165) ✦ Ruler ✦ Scrapbook or plastic flower ✦ Green pipe cleaner ✦ 3 pumpkins in graduated sizes ✦ Serrated knife ✦ Large spoon, optional ✦ Carving knife, optional ✦ 2 doorknobs ✦ 6 or 7 cabinet knobs or washers ✦ 3 drawer pulls ✦ 2 LED candles, optional

1 For hat: Use scissors to cut a rectangle out of brown felt, as tall as tomato-paste can and long enough to wrap all the way around it. Use base of can to trace a circle on brown felt; cut out circle and adhere to top of can with hot glue. Wrap felt rectangle around can and adhere with hot glue. Cut out brim template. Place template on brown felt and cut out. Use hot-glue gun to attach covered can to brim. For band, cut a 1" x 8" strip of black felt, wrap around hat and glue into place. Glue flower to pipe cleaner and tuck into hatband.

2 Cut stems off pumpkins with serrated knife. If you want to illuminate a pumpkin from within, carve a hole in top and use a large spoon to remove seeds and pulp; then carve a triangular nose. Otherwise, leave pumpkins whole.

3 For faces: Glue hardware to pumpkins. For ears, use doorknobs; for eyes, use cabinet knobs or washers mounted on circles cut from black felt; for mouths, use drawer pulls; and for noses, either use a cabinet knob or carve out a triangle (see Step 2). If using LED candles, place them inside pumpkins.

4 Stack pumpkins. Set largest pumpkin on ground or other surface, then use hot glue to attach next-largest atop it. Glue third pumpkin on top, then glue on felt hat.

Sneaky peekers

۞ ☠ ۞

YOU'LL NEED (for 1 peeping pumpkin) ✦ Serrated knife ✦ Pumpkin that fits your vessel ✦ 1 quarter, 1 dime and 1 nickel ✦ Construction paper in white and black ✦ Pencil ✦ Scissors ✦ Craft glue ✦ Covered bowl, saucepan or round casserole dish ✦ Large glue dots

1 Cut or break stem off pumpkin. Use coins as templates for eyes. For larger pumpkins, trace a quarter for the whites of eyes and a nickel for the irises; for smaller pumpkins, trace a nickel and a dime. Cut out 2 white circles and 2 black circles from construction paper. Glue circles together, then glue eyes to pumpkin.

2 Place pumpkin in vessel and top with lid. Use glue dots to help keep lid from sliding. Tilt pumpkins up or down, to achieve desired look. Note: The bottom container and the lid need not match. For the smallest pumpkin, we used two footed bowls, one for the stand and one for the hat.

DOTS
AND STRIPES

Try something different this
year by giving your pumpkins
a graphic treatment.
Here are some tips.

✦ Start with a plain
pumpkin, or spray-paint it
black or a metallic color.

✦ For dots, use a large paper
punch. To make a clean cut,
stack 10 sheets of paper and
press down on punch with
a quick, forceful motion.
Adhere dots using Mod
Podge and a brush.

✦ For stripes, use colored
duct tape or painter's tape.

Jack-o'-lantern zombies

～☠～

YOU'LL NEED (for 1 zombie) ✦ 3 pumpkins in various sizes ✦ Sharp knife ✦ Black spray paint ✦ 2 branches, each 14" long ✦ Marker ✦ 2 ³⁄₈"-diameter wooden dowels, each 3' long ✦ Drill

1 Choose pumpkins for head, body and base. Cut hole in back of head and body; hollow out. (Leave base whole.) Carve face; slice stems off body and base.

2 Spray-paint branches. On body, mark points to insert branch arms, and drill holes small enough so branches will fit tightly. (Don't insert yet.)

3 Both dowels will go in through top of body pumpkin and out through bottom. Drill a pair of holes, one on either side of stem. Insert a dowel in each and mark where they hit bottom of pumpkin. Remove dowels and drill holes in bottom, as marked. Lay pumpkin on its side and insert dowels, each through a top hole and out a bottom hole.

4 Put body on base. Mark where dowels touch top of base. Set body aside; drill holes.

5 Stack body atop base again, inserting dowels into base.

6 Mark where dowels should enter bottom of head. Drill holes and stack head on body. Insert branches in armholes.

Stenciled spiders

～☠～

YOU'LL NEED ✦ Copy machine ✦ Scissors ✦ Spider template (page 166) ✦ Pencil ✦ Black contact paper ✦ Pumpkins ✦ Spray paint in black and silver

1 Copy template in varying sizes on photocopier. Cut out.

2 Place shapes on wrong side of contact paper and trace them.

3 For black spiders on orange or spray-painted pumpkins, stick decal to pumpkin.

4 For reverse image, stick decal to pumpkin. Spray-paint entire pumpkin. Let dry. Peel off spider decal, revealing orange skin underneath.

FABULOUS FELINES

CRAFT A CABOODLE OF THE CUTEST, FRIENDLIEST KITTENS AND CATS IN TOWN

DID YOU KNOW?

At one time, it was thought that black cats served as witches' assistants, helping protect them against anyone who might try to steal their powers.

1. Kitty-cat pumpkin

✦✦✦✦✦✦✦✦✦✦✦✦✦✦✦

YOU'LL NEED ✦ Scissors ✦ Small ear template (page 167) ✦ Black construction paper ✦ Patterned scrapbook paper ✦ Craft glue ✦ Ruler ✦ Pumpkin, approximately 4" high ✦ 2 black map tacks ✦ Black fine-point marker ✦ 3 black pipe cleaners ✦ Pencil

1 Cut out ear template. Place on black paper and trace around template twice. Cut out ears. For ear inserts, cut out two slimmer 2"-high triangles from patterned paper. Glue each patterned triangle to a black ear so black border shows around pattern.

Make a ½" cut at center of ear base; fold bottom ½" of triangle toward back (nonpatterned side) flat to pumpkin surface and glue down; let dry.

2 For eyes, insert map tacks into pumpkin. For nose, cut ½"-high triangle from black paper. Position in center of pumpkin and glue in place.

3 Draw cat mouth with marker. For whiskers, cut pipe cleaners into 2½" lengths. Use a pencil to poke starter holes where you want whiskers to be. Insert pipe cleaners into holes.

2. Mama cat and kitten

✦✦✦✦✦✦✦✦✦✦✦✦✦✦✦

YOU'LL NEED ✦ Serrated knife ✦ 4 pumpkins: 1 large (about 9" diameter), 2 medium (about 6" diameter) and 1 small (about 3" diameter) ✦ Large spoon ✦ Newspaper or drop cloth ✦ Black spray paint ✦ Scissors ✦ Ruler ✦ 1¼" and ¾" hole punches, optional ✦ 1 sheet each green, black and orange construction paper or card stock ✦ Craft glue ✦ Ear templates (page 167) ✦ 1 sheet stiff black felt ✦ White chalk ✦ Sharp knife ✦ 3 wooden skewers, each 6" long ✦ Hot-glue gun ✦ White floral wire ✦ Giant chenille pipe cleaner ✦ ½"-wide orange ribbon and ⅛"-wide orange ribbon, each 1' long

1 Cut or break stems off all pumpkins. Cut a 3" circle from top of 1 of the medium pumpkins. Scoop out pulp. Use this pumpkin for large cat's head. (Other pumpkins do not need to be hollowed out.) Working over newspaper or drop cloth, spray-paint pumpkins black. Turn heads (hollowed pumpkin and small pumpkin) upside down.

2 For eyes: Using scissors or large hole punches, cut 2 1¼"-diameter circles (for large cat) and 2 ¾"-diameter circles (for small cat) out of green construction paper or card stock. To make pupils, cut 2 1¼"-long ovals (for large cat) and 2 ¾"-long ovals (for small cat), all with pointy ends, out of black construction paper or card stock. Use craft

glue to adhere black ovals to green circles, then glue eyes to heads.

3 For noses: Cut 2 triangles of orange construction paper or card stock. For large cat, sides of triangle should be 1" long; for small cat, sides should be ½" long. Glue noses to heads.

4 For ears: Cut out ear templates. Place each template on stiff black felt. Trace around each template twice. Cut out ears. Using a sharp knife, carve 2 slots in each head for ear tabs. Insert ears into heads.

5 Assemble cats: For large cat, cut 2 wooden skewers to 5" lengths and insert into bottom of hollow head on either side of hole. Center head atop large pumpkin, pushing skewers partway down into large pumpkin.

Place a bead of hot glue on top of large pumpkin, then push skewers all the way down. For small cat, break a skewer in half, insert both pieces into bottom of head and continue as with large cat, using second medium pumpkin for body.

6 For whiskers: Cut 6 4"-long pieces of white floral wire for large cat and 6 2"-long pieces for small cat. Glue whiskers to heads, 3 on each side of nose. Crinkle whiskers with your fingers.

7 For tails: Cut a 14" length of pipe cleaner and bend with your fingers. Glue to back of large cat's body. For small cat, use a 12" length.

8 For collars: Wrap ribbon around neck (use wider ribbon for mama cat). Secure in back with glue.

Terrifying tiger

❦

YOU'LL NEED ✦ Serrated knife ✦ Pumpkin, about 9" tall and 8" wide ✦ Large spoon ✦ Tiger-mask template (page 167) ✦ Scissors ✦ X-acto knife ✦ 1 sheet black craft foam ✦ White chalk ✦ Hot-glue gun ✦ Orange rickrack, 16" long ✦ Felt-tip marker ✦ Carving knife ✦ 6 regular black pipe cleaners ✦ Pair of 15-millimeter cat eyes (at suncatchereyes.com) ✦ Giant chenille pipe cleaner (at Michaels craft store) ✦ Glue dots, optional ✦ LED candle ✦ Bowl, about 5" diameter

1 Cut a 3" circle in bottom of pumpkin using serrated knife. Use spoon to remove pulp.

2 Cut out template with scissors, then cut out eyeholes with X-acto knife. Place template on craft foam and trace around it in chalk. Cut out mask with scissors and eyeholes with X-acto knife. Glue rickrack along top edge of mask; trim ends.

3 Press mask against pumpkin and trace around eyeholes with felt-tip marker. Remove mask. Cut out eyeholes on pumpkin with carving knife. Draw nose and mouth on pumpkin; carve out.

4 Glue mask to face, aligning mask eyeholes with pumpkin eyeholes. For whiskers, glue 3 regular pipe cleaners on either side of nose; trim. Use hot glue or glue dots to adhere eyes to bottom edges of eyeholes in pumpkin.

5 For ears: Cut giant chenille pipe cleaner into 2 8" lengths. Fold into triangles and glue to pumpkin on either side of stem.

6 Place LED candle on inverted bowl. Set hole in pumpkin over candle.

Creepy crawlers

❦

Paint a group of pumpkins and a bunch of small branches black. Poke little holes in the sides of the pumpkins and insert the branches to make legs. Push in yellow map tacks for eyes and then glue on triangular pieces of white paper for fangs. Use pumpkins and gourds in different shapes and sizes, and surround them on table with bowls of candy.

Carrot-nose family

❦

YOU'LL NEED ✦ **4 pumpkins in graduated sizes, for heads** ✦ **Serrated knife** ✦ **Large spoon** ✦ **2 pumpkins, small to medium size, for stands** ✦ **Hot-glue gun** ✦ **16 thumbtacks, brown or blue** ✦ **Scissors** ✦ **Black, white and patterned construction paper, 2 sheets each** ✦ **Craft glue** ✦ **Vegetable peeler** ✦ **4 small carrots** ✦ **Fishing hat** ✦ **Child-size baseball cap** ✦ **1 skein each of brown and yellow yarn** ✦ **Hardcover book, about 8" x 6"** ✦ **2 elastic ponytail holders** ✦ **2 different ribbons, each 18" long**

1 Cut a 3" circle in bottom of each pumpkin head. Scoop out pulp with a spoon.

2 Make stands: Cut both stand pumpkins in half horizontally. Discard one of the 4 halves. Cut off stems and use spoon to remove pulp. Place 3 stands on surface, cut side down. Apply hot glue around perimeter of hole on bottom of largest pumpkin head; press head onto pumpkin stand. Hold in place until secure. Repeat, leaving smallest pumpkin without a stand to make boy pumpkin.

3 For faces: Use thumbtacks for eyes, pushing points into pumpkin. For mouths, cut a crescent shape out of black construction paper and adhere to pumpkin with craft glue. (Make a larger crescent for boy's mouth.) For each nose, use sharp end of a vegetable peeler to carve a ¾" hole in center of pumpkin. Trim carrot to desired length; use peeler to shave it down until it fits into hole. Remove carrot from hole. Squeeze a bead of hot glue around nose hole of pumpkin. Insert carrot and hold in place until dry. Repeat for all pumpkins.

4 For dad pumpkin: Place fishing hat on largest pumpkin and secure with thumbtacks. For shirt collar, cut 2 triangles of white paper and adhere to stand with craft glue, just under head.

5 For boy pumpkin: Place baseball cap on smallest pumpkin. Secure with thumbtacks. Cut 2 small rectangles from white paper to make teeth. Glue to mouth.

6 For mom pumpkin: Wrap a strand of brown yarn 75 to 100 times lengthwise around book. Carefully remove entire yarn loop from book. Wrap a hair elastic around strands about ⅓ the distance from one end; cut loop at other end. Apply hot glue to stem, then attach yarn. Wrap ribbon around hair elastic and tie in bow. For shirt collar, cut 2 semicircles of patterned paper and adhere to stand with craft glue, just below head.

7 For girl pumpkin: Using yellow yarn, follow same directions as for mom's hair, but cut both ends of yarn loop. Apply hot glue around stem, then set longer yarn ponytail over stem with bangs in front. Wrap ribbon around hair elastic and tie in bow. For shirt collar, follow same steps as for mom pumpkin.

MAKE THEM LAST
Using artificial pumpkins allows you to store your decorations and display them for years to come. Check out the options at funkins.com.

Bumpkin pumpkins

~~∽◦☠◦∽~~

YOU'LL NEED (makes 1 pumpkin family) ✦ **Black construction paper** ✦ **Scissors** ✦ **Craft glue** ✦ **6 pumpkins: 3 smaller ones in graduated sizes for heads and 3 larger ones in graduated sizes for bodies** ✦ **Assortment of ribbons, buttons and yarn** ✦ **2 twist ties Hot-glue gun** ✦ **Small belt buckle** ✦ **1 small bunch natural raffia, 3" to 4" long** ✦ **2 pieces green felt** ✦ **Lightweight cardboard** ✦ **Stapler** ✦ **Chalk** ✦ **Button-front shirt with collar** ✦ **Pins**

1 Cut 3 sets of eyes and 3 mouths out of black construction paper with scissors; use craft glue to attach to pumpkin heads.

2 For baby pumpkin: Tie a length of ribbon into a bow; trim ends. Center twist tie on back of bow, attach using hot-glue gun and twist around pumpkin-head stem to secure bow.

3 To make belt, thread a length of ribbon through small belt buckle, wrap around center of pumpkin body and attach in back using hot-glue gun.

4 Secure head to body using hot-glue gun.

5 For mom pumpkin: To make hair, gather raffia bunch and secure just below one end using twist tie. Wind yarn or ribbon around twist tie until covered; tie yarn into a small bow.

6 Apply dabs of hot glue to top of pumpkin head; gently press raffia down on glue, spreading raffia out evenly. (Raffia won't cover entire top of head.)

7 Select a length of ribbon long enough to run vertically down front of pumpkin body; attach buttons along ribbon using hot-glue gun. Layer ribbon with buttons on top of a wider ribbon; secure with hot-glue gun. Attach ribbons to body using hot-glue gun.

8 Secure head to body using hot-glue gun.

9 For dad pumpkin: To make hat brim, cut a circle of felt 1½" larger in diameter than top of pumpkin head. Cut 11" x 3" rectangles out of felt and cardboard. Gently bend cardboard into tube shape to create middle of hat; staple ends together. Wrap felt around cardboard tube and secure ends with hot glue. Place tube on felt and trace around it with chalk; cut out circle. Use hot-glue gun to attach circle to one end of tube. Center open end of tube on brim and attach with hot glue.

10 Wrap ribbon around base of hat, just above brim; secure in back at hat seam using hot-glue gun. Attach hat to top of pumpkin head with hot glue.

11 Cut placket and collar from a shirt. Place it over pumpkin body; pin collar in back and secure placket with hot-glue gun.

12 Secure head to body using hot-glue gun.

TRY A NEW ANGLE
Turn the pumpkin on its side and—voilà!—the stem serves as a funny nose.

Nosy faces

≪◦ 💀 ◦≫

YOU'LL NEED ✦ Sharp serrated knife ✦ Small pumpkin with stem ✦ Miniature white pumpkin ✦ Pencil ✦ Black contact paper ✦ Scissors ✦ Printer and plain white paper ✦ Witch-hat templates (pages 168–169) ✦ Copy machine ✦ White chalk ✦ Black construction paper ✦ ½ yard black and ¼ yard orange gingham fabric ✦ Pinking shears ✦ Glue stick ✦ Hot-glue gun ✦ Ribbon and rickrack

1 Shave a slice from one side of each pumpkin to make a flat surface for it to rest on. Stand each pumpkin on its flat surface so stems face outward to become witch noses.

2 Draw eyes and mouths on back of contact paper; use scissors to cut out.

3 Remove paper liner on contact paper and affix eyes and mouths to pumpkins.

4 Use a copy machine to enlarge and reduce templates to desired sizes. Cut out templates.

5 Use chalk to trace templates on black construction paper; cut out and set aside.

6 Use chalk to trace templates on back of black and orange gingham; cut out fabric using pinking shears.

7 Glue fabric cutouts to corresponding construction paper cutouts using glue stick.

8 For each hat, fold glued fabric and paper to create hat cone; secure with hot glue.

9 Center hat cones on brims; secure with hot glue.

10 Cut a length of ribbon; tie it into a bow around base of orange hat and secure with hot glue. Cut a length of rickrack; secure it around base of black hat with hot glue. Glue hats to tops of pumpkins.

Friendly witch

≪◦ 💀 ◦≫

YOU'LL NEED ✦ Sharp serrated knife ✦ 2 small pumpkins in slightly different sizes ✦ Hot-glue gun ✦ Small bunch natural raffia, 15" long ✦ Garbage-bag twist tie ✦ Scissors ✦ 1 yard black felt ✦ Small piece red felt ✦ White glue ✦ Witch-hat templates (pages 168–169) ✦ Chalk ✦ Measuring tape ✦ Black cloth dinner napkin ✦ Cardboard or heavy card stock ✦ 1 yard decorative ribbon

1 Use knife to carefully remove both pumpkin stems. Stack small pumpkin on top of large pumpkin and glue.

2 Set aside a few pieces of raffia for witch hat. To make hair, gather raffia and secure in center with twist tie. Place gathered raffia bunch on top of witch's head; attach with hot glue. Fan out hair and trim with scissors.

3 Cut eyes out of black felt and mouth out of red felt; adhere to witch's head using white glue.

4 To make hat: If necessary, depending on your pumpkin, use a copier to enlarge template to desired size. Cut out. Trace template on black felt. Cut out.

5 Fold felt to create hat cone; secure with glue. Center hat cone on brim; secure with hot glue.

6 Wind remaining raffia around base of cone; attach with hot glue. Affix hat to pumpkin using hot glue.

7 To make cape collar, measure edge of dinner napkin. Cut a strip of cardboard that is 2" wide and 1" shorter than width of napkin.

8 Fold one edge of napkin over cardboard strip; use dabs of hot glue to hold collar in place.

9 Drape cape around witch's body, securing in place with hot-glue gun.

10 Tie decorative ribbon just beneath collar of cape.

Haunt your house

Send chills up the spine of trick-or-treaters and passersby with spooky decorations for your front door, porch and yard.

Doors & windows

Welcome ghouls and goblins with a suitably spooky door, and scare away nosy ghosts with windows that stare back. These projects send out a clear message: The spirit of Halloween is alive and well at this house!

Witchy doorbell

ᥫᩣ💀ᥫᩣ

YOU'LL NEED ✦ Scissors ✦ Black foam sheet ✦ Craft glue ✦ Large button ✦ Black and natural raffia ✦ Large toothpick ✦ Marker ✦ Orange paper ✦ Double-sided tape

1 Cut witch's cape and hat out of foam sheet. For head, glue button to top of cape. Cut short lengths of black raffia for hair; glue raffia to button. Glue on hat. Glue a piece of black raffia to hat as a band.

2 Cut natural raffia for broom and glue it on to end of toothpick; glue toothpick to witch. Write *Push if you dare* on orange paper. Cut out and glue in place.

Trick-or-treat sign

ᥫᩣ💀ᥫᩣ

YOU'LL NEED ✦ X-acto knife ✦ Orange foam core ✦ Awl ✦ 18-gauge wire or small sharp point ✦ Wire ✦ Computer with printer ✦ Craft glue

1 Cut 3 pumpkin shapes out of foam core. Punch a small hole through top of each and slide wire through. Thread wire through screen door to secure in place.

2 Type and print letters; stick to foam-core pumpkins with glue.

PARK HERE
Take an umbrella stand, fill it with straw brooms and add a chalkboard sign so witches know what to do.

TRICK

OR

TREAT

LEAVE
BROOMS
HERE

BOO

Furry door

༄◦💀◦༄

YOU'LL NEED
✦ Eye templates (page 170) ✦ Copy machine ✦ Scissors ✦ Measuring tape ✦ 4 to 6 yards black fake fur (at fabric or craft stores), depending on door size ✦ Transparent tape ✦ White marker or crayon ✦ 10 sheets 8½" x 11" paper in neon colors ✦ Duct tape ✦ 1 or 2 sheets black construction paper ✦ Double-sided tape ✦ 8 3M Command strips

1 On copy machine, enlarge eye templates to various sizes, as desired. (Largest is 400 percent.) Make 10 pairs and cut out.

2 Measure door; cut fur to size. Place fabric, fur side down, on flat surface. Position eye templates on back of fabric, leaving room to accommodate door handle; temporarily tape them in place.

3 Outline each eye template on back of fabric with marker; remove templates and discard. Cut out eye openings.

4 Cover back of each eye opening with neon paper; secure with duct tape. Turn fabric over, fur side up. Cut circles for pupils from black paper. Use double-sided tape to secure a pupil to each eye.

5 Turn fur wrong side up. Apply 2 strips of duct tape along each edge. Apply 3M Command strips as follows: 1 in each corner, 1 at center of top edge and 2 along each side edge. Holding top edge of fur, position over door. Press to make fur adhere securely to surface.

6 Cut a hole in fabric to accommodate handle of door.

ALL-EYES WINDOWS

Use an X-acto knife to cut eyes out of 2 large sheets of black construction paper. Back each with orange wrapping paper, then affix to windows.

Screaming door face

✎☠✎

YOU'LL NEED ✦ **Eye template (page 171)** ✦ **Scissors** ✦ **Pencil** ✦ **Orange and white poster board, 1 sheet each** ✦ **Measuring tape** ✦ **Black and red construction paper** ✦ **White glue** ✦ **Removable double-sided poster tape**

1 Cut out eye template. Trace onto orange poster board twice and cut out.

2 Cut about 20 triangles out of white poster board, ranging in length from 5" to 10".

3 Measure door; cut black paper to be several inches larger. (If using two pieces of paper, place seam at center so mouth covers it.)

4 Lay black paper flat on floor. For mouth, cut piece of red paper 3" to 4" wider than door and about ⅓ the door's length. Position mouth slightly lower than center. Set eyes above mouth, tilted inward for a scarier look. Add white triangles as teeth, placing longest fangs first, then filling in. Glue pieces in place.

5 Adhere entire face to door with double-sided poster tape.

The wreath has eyes

✎☠✎

YOU'LL NEED ✦ **Black floral spray paint** ✦ **24 silk flowers** ✦ **Assorted artificial foliage** ✦ **14" straw wreath form** ✦ **1"-wide black grosgrain ribbon, 8 yards** ✦ **Hot-glue gun** ✦ **8 pairs of googly eyes in various sizes**

1 Spray-paint flowers and foliage. Let dry. Wrap wreath form in ribbon. Secure ends with glue.

2 Glue flowers and foliage to form, starting with larger blooms. Glue pairs of eyes to wreath.

903

HANG CRAWLING SPIDERS

Invert an oval platter (for body) and a salad plate (for head) on a large sheet of black paper; trace around and cut out. Draw 8 legs and a pair of pincers freehand and cut out. Make web by sticking thick yarn to the door with tape.

PORE
JUD
IS
DAID

RIP
SLIM

CLIFF
DIVER
IN PIECES

Porches

Set the stage for fright night. Let these large-scale crafts transform your porch area into a theater of eerie delights. With decorations this sensational, your neighbors might wonder just what has possessed you.

Pumpkin man
❧☠❧

YOU'LL NEED ✦ **10 to 12 magazines** ✦ **Newspapers** ✦ **Masking tape or duct tape** ✦ **Clothing: long-sleeve shirt, overalls or pants, boots, hat** ✦ **Chair** ✦ **Monster gloves (at costume stores)** ✦ **Carved pumpkin** ✦ **Dowel, optional** ✦ **Mop head**

1 To create a skeleton, open 1 magazine to middle and wrap around rolled-up newspaper; wrapped roll should be the diameter of an arm. Wrap in tape to secure. Make 4 arm-size pieces and 4 leg-size rolls. Wad newspaper into 4 balls to make knees and elbows.

2 For torso, open 1 magazine to middle and lay flat. Place wadded newspaper on top. Place a second open magazine atop newspaper; wrap tape around entire bundle.

3 Layer clothes (pull overalls over shirt, for instance). Insert body parts into clothes. Arrange body in chair and fill in clothing with wadded newspaper as desired. Tuck monster gloves into shirtsleeves. Tuck pant legs into boots.

4 Place carved pumpkin atop torso of monster. If it feels unstable, insert dowel through bottom of pumpkin and down through torso. Add mop head for hair. Top with hat.

Porch pillar trees
❧☠❧

YOU'LL NEED ✦ **Measuring tape** ✦ **Craft paper** ✦ **Brown paint in 2 shades, 1 darker and 1 lighter than craft paper** ✦ **Paintbrushes** ✦ **Brown twine** ✦ **Duct tape or masking tape** ✦ **Double-sided clear tape**

1 Measure porch pillars; add 1' to that measurement and cut 2 pieces of craft paper to that length. Also cut 3 16"-long pieces of craft paper.

2 Lay pieces of paper flat on ground. Starting with darker shade of brown, paint wavy vertical stripes along length of paper, imitating look of bark. Use some heavier strokes and some lighter ones. An old, stiff, dried-out paintbrush works well for this.

3 Repeat process using lighter brown paint, but don't cover craft paper completely with paint—brown paper should show through in places.

4 Set aside 16" lengths of paper. Working on pillar-length pieces, crumple from top to bottom, then uncrumple. Take side edge and fold, accordion-style, in 2" or 3" pleats. Continue until completely folded, then twist tightly.

5 Carefully unfold. Wrap each pillar with two pieces of paper. Use twine and tape to secure.

6 To make roots, twist 16" pieces, 1 at a time, to form funnel shape. One end of funnel should be very tight and the other very loose. Starting at the tight end, tie with twine every 4" or 5", leaving about 4" on the more open end. Using double-sided tape, attach 3 roots to base of each tree.

Bat storm

❧ ☠ ❧

YOU'LL NEED ✦ **Copy machine** ✦ **Bat templates (page 172)** ✦ **Scissors** ✦ **Craft foam (a 9" x 12" sheet yields 2 standard bats; for larger bats, use 12" x 18" sheet)** ✦ **Pencil** ✦ **Pushpin** ✦ **Nylon fishing line**

1 To make different-size bats, use copy machine to reduce template to 60 percent or enlarge to 150 percent. Cut out.

2 Cut 9" x 12" sheet of craft foam in half lengthwise to make two pieces, each 4½" x 12".

3 Fold one piece in half crosswise, so it measures 4½" x 6". Crease. Place template along crease and trace onto foam. Keeping craft foam folded, cut out bat shape, cutting through both layers of foam. (Tip: If you're having trouble keeping foam in place while you cut, staple outside corners together.) Unfold.

4 Hang bats. There are several options. • Use pushpin to make hole in each bat and feed fishing line through hole. Tie 1 end in a double knot so it won't slip back through. • Threading line through center of bat will make it hang evenly. Place hole closer to head, and head will hang higher than body. • To bring wings closer together, make a hole in each wing and use 1 piece of fishing line as a cross-wire (double-knot it on both ends). Attach the cross-wire across the back of the bat to bring wings up. Creating a cross-wire underneath the bat will make wings hang down.

Ginormous spider

❧ ☠ ❧

YOU'LL NEED ✦ **Water-based spray paint, black** ✦ **8"- to 10"-diameter Styrofoam ball** ✦ **3 6' lengths of foam pipe insulation** ✦ **Scissors** ✦ **Black telephone or stereo wires or twine** ✦ **Hot-glue gun** ✦ **White paper, cardboard or foam** ✦ **Nylon fishing line**

1 Spray-paint Styrofoam ball black. Let dry. For 6 rear legs: Cut 6 2' pieces of pipe insulation. Bend each in half. Bind fold with wire to make knee. Measure 5" from 1 end, fold insulation and bind fold with wire to make ankle. For 2 front legs, cut 2 10" lengths of pipe insulation. Measure 4" from 1 end, fold insulation and bind fold with wire.

2 Working on thigh (longer part) of each leg, snip end diagonally so it fits snugly against the ball. Starting with front legs, glue each leg to ball. (Refer to photo for positioning.)

3 Cut 2 half-circles, about 3" across, out of white paper, cardboard or craft foam. Cut a thin crosswise slice of pipe insulation. Cut it in half to make 2 C-shaped pieces; glue 1 on each half-circle. Glue each eye on ball. To hang spider, tie fishing line around legs.

Terrifying tombstones

YOU'LL NEED ✦ Sharp knife ✦ Foam, 2" thick x 18" wide and 10" to 24" long ✦ Black ballpoint pen or marker ✦ Utility knife ✦ Chopstick or unsharpened pencil ✦ Distressing tool: knife, needle-nose pliers or fork ✦ Paintbrushes: 1 small with point, 1 flat, 2" to 3" ✦ Gray paint ✦ Darker gray paint, plus sponge or rag, optional ✦ Handsaw ✦ Pair of ½"-diameter dowels, each 2' long ✦ Hammer

1 Use knife to cut tombstone shape out of foam. Write inscription and draw design on front of tombstone.

2 To "engrave" letters, use utility knife to slice along right side of pen mark at 45-degree angle, then repeat on left side of pen mark. (Slices should meet in center, leaving V-shaped sliver of foam you can remove.) When all letters are engraved, drag chopstick through each groove to roughen it up.

3 Distress tombstone. Depending on foam type used, you can slice off pieces with knife, pull away hunks with needle-nose pliers, or scrape away surface of foam with fork.

4 Using small brush, paint inside each groove and over any area you've scraped or broken away.

5 Using flat brush, paint tombstone front, back and sides. If desired, apply darker color for texture, using sponge, rag or fingers.

6 Using saw, cut one end of each dowel into a point. Insert pointed ends of each dowel straight into bottom of tombstone.

7 Position tombstone in your yard, marking where dowels should go. Remove dowels from tombstone, and hammer pointed ends about 1' into ground. Slide tombstone over dowels.

Yards &
walkways

Leave a scary display where
visitors least expect to see one.

Witch legs and ruby slippers

꩜💀꩜

YOU'LL NEED ✦ Newspaper ✦ Red spray paint ✦ Ladies' pumps (slip-ons work best) ✦ Paintbrush ✦ Glue ✦ Red glitter ✦ Scissors ✦ Measuring tape ✦ 1 sheet red paper ✦ Clear packing tape ✦ 4 shoelaces ✦ 2 pieces pipe insulation, each about 21" long ✦ 2 magazines ✦ 6 sheets white paper ✦ Black-and-white-striped knee- or thigh-high socks

1 Cover floor with newspaper and spray-paint shoes red (including soles). Let dry. Working over newspaper, brush glue onto shoes (excluding soles) in sections and sprinkle with glitter. Let dry.

2 To make bows, cut 2 1" x 7" strips from red paper. Take both ends of 1 strip; fold in so ends meet in middle. Tape to secure. Repeat with other strip. Working over newspaper, brush bows with glue and sprinkle with glitter. Glue a bow to toe of each shoe.

3 To make foot, tie shoelace 7" from end of pipe insulation; cinch tight. To make ankle, tie second shoelace 1½" up from first shoelace; cinch tight. Remaining insulation will be leg. Bend insulation at ankle to form an L shape; tape in place. Repeat to make second leg.

4 Wrap 2 newspaper sheets around each foot; tape in place. Wrap an entire magazine around each leg; tape in place. Crumple 2 newspaper sheets and tape 1 behind each ankle to create heels. Cut ends of both feet into a V shape.

5 Wrap white paper around legs and feet; tape in place. Pull socks over feet and up legs, tucking excess into insulation. Slide feet into shoes.

6 Pick an outdoor spot that allows legs' unfinished ends to abut a building or be tucked out of sight (such as next to a garage, staircase or shrub). Position legs in selected location with feet sticking out.

FRIENDLY FIENDS

WHO SAYS SPOOKY CAN'T BE CUTE? HERE'S A SKULL AND GHOSTS TO MAKE YOU SMILE.

HANG IT UP

To display flying ghost (left), thread a needle with fishing line and take several stitches through top of ghost's head. Remove needle and tie ends of line together to form a loop.

1. Skull piñata

✦✦✦✦✦✦✦✦✦✦✦✦✦✦✦

YOU'LL NEED
✦ **1 cup flour**
✦ **½ teaspoon salt**
✦ **2 cups water** ✦ **Large bowl** ✦ **Newspaper**
✦ **Balloon, blown up and tied** ✦ **Ribbon** ✦ **Scissors**
✦ **Masking tape** ✦ **Candy**
✦ **Paintbrush** ✦ **White glow-in-the-dark paint** ✦ **Black marker**

1 Place flour and salt in bowl and add water slowly, stirring. Tear newspaper into strips. Dip strips into mixture; remove excess paste. Lay strips on balloon and smooth. Cover balloon, leaving a small hole at bottom (around knot). Let dry.

2 Run ribbon vertically around piñata. Loop ribbon at top and cut off excess; secure with tape. This will be your hanger.

3 Add two more layers of papier-mâché over balloon and ribbon ends. Let dry between layers. Use scissors to pop

balloon, then remove it through opening.

4 Fill piñata with candy. Tape over opening, then cover tape with papier-mâché. Let dry. Paint balloon; let dry. Use marker to draw skull eyes, teeth, nostrils and cracks. Hang from loop.

2. Ghostly twins

✦✦✦✦✦✦✦✦✦✦✦✦✦✦✦

YOU'LL NEED (for 1 ghost) ✦ **2 ¾"-diameter dowels, 3' long for boy, 2' long for girl** ✦ **Pants: 3T for boy, 2T for girl**
✦ **Newspaper** ✦ **Pair of socks** ✦ **String**
✦ **8"-diameter Styrofoam ball** ✦ **54" square of white fabric** ✦ **Black felt** ✦ **Glue**

1 Slide 1 pant leg over each dowel. Position dowels where you want figures to stand; push dowels into ground about 6" apart.

2 Fill pants and socks with crumpled newspaper. Lift pant legs and tie top of each sock to

a dowel with string, at the ankle. Pull pant legs over tops of socks, and arrange stuffed socks in front to look like feet.

3 Insert dowel ends into a Styrofoam ball, about 2" to 3" apart. Drape white fabric over head and arrange as

desired. Cut 2 3" ovals out of felt for eyes; glue in place.

4 Accessorize. For instance, give the boy ghost a trick-or-treat bag; attach it with a clothespin clipped underneath white fabric. For girl ghost, glue a bow to top of head.

3. Flying ghost

✦✦✦✦✦✦✦✦✦✦✦✦✦✦✦

YOU'LL NEED
✦ **Wire cutters** ✦ **Baling wire** ✦ **3'-tall vase**
✦ **8"-diameter foam ball**
✦ **Drop cloth** ✦ **Measuring tape** ✦ **6 yards cheesecloth**
✦ **Scissors** ✦ **1 16-oz. bottle fabric stiffener** ✦ **Bucket**
✦ **Black felt** ✦ **Hot-glue gun** ✦ **Fishing line**
✦ **Needle**

1 Make a form for molding cheesecloth. Cut a 3' piece of baling wire. Fold in half, then shape each half into a downward curve. Fold ends upward to form hands. Tape wire to vase, which will serve as a form for the body so arms wrap

around to front. Place vase on drop cloth. Place ball on vase.

2 Cut 4 lengths of cheesecloth long enough to completely cover form with 4" extra all the way around.

3 Pour fabric stiffener into bucket. Dip

cheesecloth, one piece at a time, into liquid, then drape piece over form. Repeat with each piece of fabric. Let dry.

4 Cut 2 small oval eyes and 1 large oval mouth of black felt. Glue them to face. Remove cheesecloth from form.

Mailbox monster

ༀ☠ༀ

YOU'LL NEED ✦ **2 shoelaces** ✦ **Measuring tape** ✦ **Pipe insulation, 8" longer than mailbox height** ✦ **Newspaper** ✦ **Duct tape** ✦ **Man's shirt** ✦ **Monster glove (at costume shops)** ✦ **18" wooden dowel** ✦ **Hammer** ✦ **Fishing line** ✦ **Scissors** ✦ **Safety pins**

1 To make forearm, tie shoelace 12" from end of insulation; cinch. For elbow, tie second shoelace 4" up from first; cinch. Remaining insulation will be upper arm.

2 Wrap newspaper around upper arm and forearm; secure with tape. Create elbow using balled-up newspaper; tape to insulation. Slide arm through shirtsleeve. Slip glove onto arm. Tape glove to newspaper.

3 Position dowel 4" to 6" in front of mailbox post. Angle dowel away from post; use hammer to drive dowel into ground. Slide upper arm onto dowel. Bend elbow and position palm under mailbox.

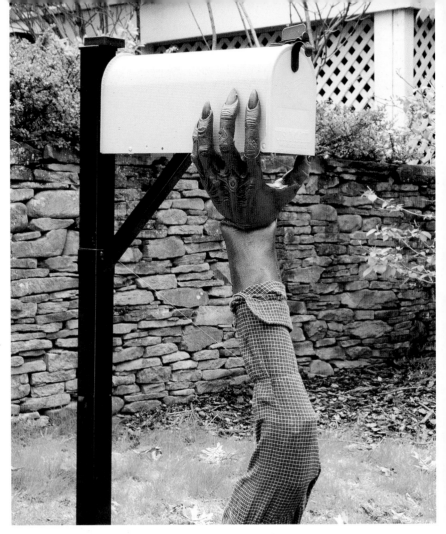

4 Slide fishing line through mounting hole on side of mailbox. Tie around pointer finger to keep hand in place.

Wrap shirt around arm base to hide newspaper; pin in place. Pile dirt and leaves around base.

Witchy luminarias

ༀ☠ༀ

YOU'LL NEED ✦ **Copy machine** ✦ **Witch and moon templates (page 173)** ✦ **Scissors** ✦ **3 orange paper bags (at party supply stores)** ✦ **Tape** ✦ **3 votive candles** ✦ **3 glass votive holders**

1 Make 3 copies each of witch and moon templates. Cut out shapes, following image outline as closely as possible.

2 Tape a moon shape in upper-right-hand corner of each bag. Center a witch inside one bag and tape in place. On second bag, position a witch almost directly below moon. Tape in place, folding bristle end of broom around side of bag. This bag will go at right. On third bag, position a witch to left of moon, so she appears to be flying off left-hand edge of bag.

3 Place each candle in a holder. Light, then set in bag. (If you're using luminarias outdoors, fill bottoms with sand.)

CAT WALK

LEAVE A CAT-PRINT TRAIL

Make visitors wonder just how large a kitty-cat you have! Cut out giant paw pads and toes from black contact paper. Remove backing paper and arrange cutouts on walkway. For sign, paint a piece of wood orange and let dry completely. Rip pieces of tape off roll, leaving edges jagged, and spell out *cat walk*. Tape a border around sign. Spray-paint entire board black and remove tape once paint is dry.

Decorate your digs

Whether you want to give your home an eerie glow or celebrate the season in a more subdued fashion, here are loads of ideas and inspiration to help you set the mood.

Spooky decorations

Transform your rooms with bewitching projects. Mysteriously easy yet wickedly attractive, these crafts are certain to add a spine-tingling thrill to your décor.

Ghoulish garland

YOU'LL NEED ✦ **Orange, black and white crepe paper, 1 roll each** ✦ **Scissors** ✦ **Scotch tape** ✦ **Pumpkin, bat and ghost templates (page 174)** ✦ **White, black and orange construction paper** ✦ **X-acto knife** ✦ **Darning needle** ✦ **Orange yarn**

1 Measure mantel. Cut 1 strand of orange, black and white crepe paper, each twice as long as mantel. Tape ends of crepe paper to end of mantel and loosely braid strands. Tape to mantel every 1' for swag effect.

2 Cut out templates. Use X-acto knife to cut out facial features. Calculate how many ornaments you'll need (figuring 1 for every 6"). Place templates on paper; trace around them, including outline of facial features. Repeat until you have desired number of ornaments. Cut out, using X-acto knife for facial features. Thread needle with yarn. Insert needle through top of an ornament and string yarn through. Cut yarn and tie to form loop. Tape loop to mantel underneath garland. Repeat.

Bat pillow

YOU'LL NEED ✦ **12" x 12" pillow with removable cover** ✦ **1 yard orange felt** ✦ **Ruler** ✦ **Marker** ✦ **Scissors** ✦ **Fabric glue** ✦ **Bat template (page 174)** ✦ **¼ yard black felt** ✦ **Orange paper** ✦ **Double-sided tape**

1 Remove cover from pillow. Trace cover on orange felt, adding ½ inch to each side. Trace cover on orange felt a second time, adding a triangular flap along one side (to make the shape of a house). Cut out both pieces. Lay pieces on top of each other and use fabric glue to seal three edges, leaving edge with flap open. Let dry completely. Turn inside out.

2 Cut out template and place on black felt. Trace around. Repeat twice. Cut out and glue bats to front of pillowcase. Let dry. Insert pillow and tuck in flap.

♦♦♦♦♦♦♦♦♦♦♦♦♦♦♦♦

GIVE THE ROOM A GLOW

Carve jack-o'-lantern faces into peat pots, using an X-acto knife. Try a different face on each pot. Line pots up in a row. Place votives in glass holders inside pots and light candles.

Tin-can lantern

☙ 💀 ↄ

YOU'LL NEED (for 1 lantern) ✦ **Tin can, empty, clean and dry** ✦ **Water** ✦ **Pumpkin template (page 174)** ✦ **Copier** ✦ **Tape** ✦ **Hammer** ✦ **Nail** ✦ **Votive candle**

1 Fill can with water. Place in freezer and leave until frozen.

2 With copier, size pumpkin template to fit and tape it to can. Use hammer and medium-size nail to punch holes around the design, plus eyes, nose and mouth. Defrost frozen can in sink so water can run out. Dry can. Place votive candle inside and light it.

Haunted dollhouse

≈❦≈

YOU'LL NEED ✦ **Black Krylon Fusion for Plastic spray paint** ✦ **Dollhouse** ✦ **12 ice-pop sticks** ✦ **Scissors**
✦ **1 sheet of amber cellophane** ✦ **Hot-glue gun** ✦ **2 large pinecones** ✦ **Dried Spanish moss** ✦ **Dried or artificial**
flowers ✦ **Marker** ✦ **String of small white Christmas lights** ✦ **2 small brown paper bags**

1 Apply 2 coats of spray paint to house (inside and out) and to 8 ice-pop sticks.

2 Cut squares or rectangles of cellophane slightly larger than each window. Working from inside dollhouse, glue cellophane to window frames.

3 Carefully break scales off pinecones. Use hot glue to attach a single row of scales to edge of roof to look like shingles. Decorate dollhouse exterior by gluing Spanish moss and flowers in place.

4 Board up windows and doors with black ice-pop sticks. Glue in place. Use remainder of ice-pop sticks to make KEEP OUT and BEWARE signs. String lights inside house. To make trees, cut tops off paper bags. Twist bags. Cut tops into strips. Crumple strips.

Googly-eyed spiders

෨ঔ☠෨ঔ

YOU'LL NEED ✦ Scissors ✦ 12 empty 9-oz. water bottles ✦ Drill with ⅛" bit ✦ Black spray paint ✦ Black string or raffia ✦ Craft glue ✦ 24 mini googly eyes ✦ Masking tape

1 Cut bottom off of each bottle, leaving 4" to 6" for legs. Cut remaining portion of bottle vertically into 8 leg strips.

2 Drill hole through top of each cap. Screw cap onto a bottle. Spray-paint bottle and let dry.

3 Glue a pair of eyes to each bottle's cap.

4 Cut 12 pieces of string, each 2' to 3' long. Knot one end; thread other through hole in cap, working from inside bottle.

5 Tape end of string to ceiling.

Kitty-cat treat bags

෨ঔ☠෨ঔ

YOU'LL NEED ✦ Lunch bags ✦ Pencil ✦ Scissors ✦ Orange paper ✦ Craft glue ✦ Black marker ✦ Toothpick ✦ Raffia ✦ Tape

1 Starting 6" from bottom of a bag, use pencil to draw outline of top of a cat's head so that ears are at sides of bag. Cut off top of bag along outline.

2 Cut a small triangle of orange paper for nose; glue to center of face. Draw eyes and mouth in black marker.

3 For whiskers, poke 3 holes on each side of nose with toothpick. Cut 3 lengths of raffia, each 8" long. Thread raffia through holes to form whiskers across face. Tape from behind, inside bag. Trim whiskers as needed.

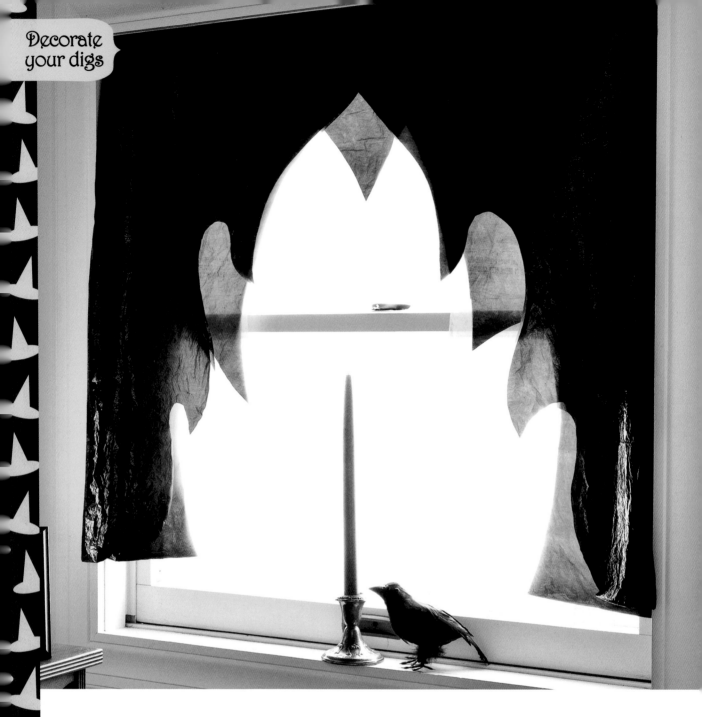

Eerie window treatment

✁❦✁

YOU'LL NEED ✦ Black plastic trash bag, large enough to cover window ✦ Scissors ✦ Painter's tape
✦ White grease pencil or crayon ✦ Double-sided tape

1 If trash bag has built-in cinch or ties, cut straight across top to remove. Cut open sides and bottom to make two pieces of equal size. Tape one piece over window, securing it tightly on all four sides.

2 Draw a simple design that resembles curtains and a valance. It does not need to be perfectly symmetrical. Remove tape and cut out shape. Tape other piece of plastic to a flat surface, then tape cut-out shape on top of it.

Draw a similar, slightly larger shape on second piece. There should be some areas where shapes overlap and others where they don't. (This helps give depth to the curtains.) Remove tape. Crumple each piece several times. This helps to disguise creases in trash bags.

3 Secure top and sides of larger piece to inside of window frame with double-sided tape. Tape remaining piece to window frame, on top of first.

Creepy lanterns

☙ 💀 ❧

YOU'LL NEED ✦ Computer with printer and paper ✦ Copy machine ✦ Spider template (page 166) ✦ Black tissue paper ✦ Orange paper lanterns ✦ Craft glue

1 For letters, type EEK and BOO on your computer in a large font size (try 700-point). Print letters; cut out. For spider lantern, copy template, enlarging or reducing it as needed. Cut out spiders.

2 Place templates on tissue paper and cut out. Glue tissue paper letters and shapes to lanterns.

FRIGHTEN THE FOLKS
Copy or scan and print family photos in black and white, then cut small fangs out of white card stock and attach them to the photos with a glue stick. Display pictures around the house to give guests an unexpected jolt.

Creepy-crawlers candleholders

❧☠❧

YOU'LL NEED ✦ Scissors ✦ White vellum paper ✦ Water glasses ✦ Spider stamp ✦ Ink pad ✦ Double-sided tape ✦ Votive candle

1 Cut strips of vellum to fit around water glasses. Embellish vellum strips with spider stamp.

2 Secure paper around each glass with double-sided tape. Place a votive candle inside.

Halloween mobile

❧☠❧

YOU'LL NEED ✦ Scissors ✦ Pumpkin, ghost and bat templates (page 175) ✦ 8½" x 11" sheets of orange, yellow, white and black or gray vellum paper, 5 of each color ✦ Pencil ✦ Cutting mat ✦ X-acto knife ✦ ⅛" and ¼" hole punches ✦ Embroidery thread or dental floss ✦ ½"-diameter dowel rod, 18" long

1 Cut out pumpkin, ghost and bat templates with scissors.

2 For pumpkins: Place template on orange vellum, trace twice with pencil and cut out 2 pumpkins. Trace once on yellow vellum; cut out shape. Place orange pumpkins on cutting mat; cut out facial features with X-acto knife. For ghosts: Place template on white vellum, trace twice and cut out 2 ghosts. Trace once on gray vellum; cut out shape. Use ¼" hole punch to make eyes on white ghosts. For bats: Place template on black or gray vellum, trace twice and cut out 2 bats. Trace once on yellow vellum; cut out shape. Then use ⅛" hole punch and cut out eyes on black or gray bats.

3 Stack the 3 layers of each ornament—note that middle layer does not have facial features. Use ⅛" punch to make a hole at top. Insert an 18" length of thread through that hole and knot to secure.

4 Tie ornaments to dowel, arranging them so they hang at different lengths and don't overlap one another. (For a feeling of greater dimension, cross 2 dowels in an X shape, using tape at the intersecting point to keep rods in place.) Trim excess thread. Hang mobile near a window so light can pass through.

Spooky trees

❧ 💀 ☙

YOU'LL NEED ✦ **Black tree template (page 176)** ✦ **Copier** ✦ **Scissors** ✦ **Glue stick** ✦ **Black marker**

1 For each tree, make 3 copies of tree template. Cut out.

2 Fold each tree in half lengthwise, black side folded in. Cover white side of each tree with glue. Align trees so that all 3 fold lines meet, then press together so that trunks and branches adhere to one another. Color in any exposed white area with black marker.

Chalkboard candleholders

❧ 💀 ☙

YOU'LL NEED ✦ **Smooth-sided glass cylinders or jars in various sizes** ✦ **Painter's tape** ✦ **Black chalkboard spray paint** ✦ **Chalk** ✦ **Rag** ✦ **Votive candle**

1 For each candleholder, decide where you want to paint chalkboard band on jar, then mask remainder of glass with painter's tape.

2 Apply three coats of chalkboard spray paint. Let dry thoroughly after each coat.

3 Remove tape. Write on paint with chalk, then erase with rag to create a dust coating. Write words or draw designs on top of dust coating. Place candles inside jar.

Mummy balls

⚡💀⚡

YOU'LL NEED (for 1 mummy ball) ✦ **2 or 3 white paper towels** ✦ **Spray starch** ✦ **Scissors**
✦ **Black electrical tape (or white masking tape and a black marker to color)** ✦ **1 orange**
✦ **Transparent tape** ✦ **Double-sided tape** ✦ **Glue** ✦ **Googly eyes**

1 Wet 2 or 3 paper towels; wring out and unfold. Spray towels with starch until evenly saturated. Let dry. Stick 3" length of black tape on side of orange to create background for eyes.

2 Wrap a dried paper towel around orange, covering all fruit; leave black tape exposed. Secure paper towel with transparent tape.

3 Tear remaining paper towels into strips, each about 1" x 6". Place 1 strip vertically across center of black

tape to form space between eyes. Attach to orange using transparent tape.

4 Wrap paper towel strips around orange, securing with double-sided tape as you go. Some strips will overlap or have loose ends—this adds to the mummy effect. Tear edges of strips to make them jagged.

5 Glue googly eyes in place atop black tape. Completed balls look best in a group. They can be displayed on top of candlesticks or in a footed bowl as a centerpiece.

Decorate
your digs

Clip-on bats

⁓💀⁓

YOU'LL NEED (makes 8 bats)
✦ **Scissors** ✦ **Small bat template (page 172)** ✦ **Pencil** ✦ **Black construction paper, 8 sheets** ✦ **8 wooden clothespins** ✦ **Wooden dowel** ✦ **Black spray paint** ✦ **Double-sided tape**

1 Cut out bat template. Fold each sheet of construction paper in half. Place template on fold and trace around twice; cut out 16 bats.

2 Clip clothespins to dowel. In a well-ventilated area, hold dowel and spray-paint clothespins black, rotating for even coverage. Let dry.

3 Remove pins from dowel. Put double-sided tape on one side of each clothespin. Repeat for all. Center 1 bat on tape; press to stick.

4 Turn each bat over so clothespin is on top. Put double-sided tape on each wing tip.

5 Put piece of double-sided tape on exposed side of clothespin. Center other bat on tape; press to stick. Press tips of bats' wings together; repeat for each clothespin.

CAPTURE A SPIRIT
Draw a ghost on white tissue paper and cut it out, using an X-acto knife for the face. Loosely tape to inside of jar.

Witchy candy jars

⁓💀⁓

YOU'LL NEED ✦ **Scissors** ✦ **Witch-hat and brim template (pages 168–169)** ✦ **Construction paper in black, purple and yellow** ✦ **Pencil** ✦ **Double-sided tape** ✦ **Craft glue** ✦ **Jars with lids (2¾"-diameter lids will fit hat template)** ✦ **Candy** ✦ **Paper punch**

1 Cut out templates. Place templates on black construction paper; trace shapes and cut out.

2 Create cone shape for top of witch hat; tape seam. Bend tabs of brim upward and glue to inside of cone. Cut a crescent shape out of colored paper. Glue it to front of hat.

3 To make hair, cut 2 2" x 4" pieces of black paper. Cut ¼"-wide strips along length of paper, leaving fringe attached at one end. To curl, carefully run each strip between your thumb and a scissor blade.

4 Tape hair to inside of hat. Place a bead of glue around inside edge of hat, and fit hat over jar lid.

5 Fill jar with candy of choice (face will show up better with light-color candy) and screw on lid. For face: Cut two half-ovals, a carrot-shaped nose and a crooked smile out of black paper. Use paper punch to make two dots from yellow construction paper, then glue a dot to each half-oval to make eyes. Crumple nose to give it texture, then unfold. Glue all facial features to jar.

INCREDIBLE EDIBLES
USE SWEETS AND SNACKS TO MAKE THESE DELECTABLE DECORATIONS.

PROTECT YOUR PET

Take care to keep the decorations out of reach of your family's dog or cat. Candy—chocolate in particular—can make animals sick.

1. Hanging hands

◆◆◆◆◆◆◆◆◆◆◆◆◆◆◆

YOU'LL NEED
✦ **Assorted small candies or snack foods (cheese puffs, M&M's, jelly beans)** ✦ **Clear plastic glove** ✦ **Ribbon, 1' to 3' long** ✦ **Scissors** ✦ **Masking tape**

1 Drop 1 piece of candy into each fingertip of glove to create fingernails. Fill rest of glove with candy in a contrasting color.

2 Knot wrist of glove (as if tying a balloon). Tie end of ribbon to glove, and leave other end free. To hang, tape end of ribbon to door or wall.

> **For a colorful display make several of these, filling each glove with a different type of candy.**

2. Topiary trees

◆◆◆◆◆◆◆◆◆◆◆◆◆◆◆◆

YOU'LL NEED (for 1 cone) ✦ **Hot-glue gun** ✦ **Styrofoam cone** ✦ **1"-wide ribbon, about 2 yards** ✦ **Assorted candies (candy corn, gumdrops, black licorice, jelly rings)** ✦ **Packaged cobweb** ✦ **Plastic spiders**

1 Glue end of ribbon to base of cone, and, working upward, wrap entire cone, gluing to attach as you work.

2 Starting at base of cone, glue on candy. Create a striped effect by alternating rows of different types of candy. Continue until cone is completely covered.

3 Wrap a fine layer of cobweb over cone. Add plastic spiders, gluing each in place.

3. Sweet globes

◆◆◆◆◆◆◆◆◆◆◆◆◆◆◆◆

YOU'LL NEED
✦ **Styrofoam balls** ✦ **Black spray paint** ✦ **Assorted candies (Reese's Pieces, candy corn, black gumdrops, jelly rings, Skittles)** ✦ **Low-temperature glue gun**

1 Spray Styrofoam balls with black paint. Let dry.

2 Glue candy to balls in a uniform pattern, working in concentric circles around entire ball. Let glue dry completely before displaying.

> **Use a pedestal to show off these decorations. Shiny drinking glasses, candlesticks and bowls all make attractive stands.**

◆◆◆◆◆◆◆◆◆◆◆◆◆

HALLOWEEN FACTS

Jack-o'-lanterns started as an Irish tradition, but in Ireland, instead of carving pumpkins, they hollow out oversize rutabagas, turnips and potatoes. Using pumpkins is a North American custom.

✦ ✦ ✦

Trick-or-treating evolved from the ancient Celtic practice of putting out treats and food as an offering to spirits that roamed the streets at Samhain, a sacred festival that marked the end of the Celtic calendar year.

✦ ✦ ✦

Halloween has been called All Hallows' Eve, Witches Night, Snap-Apple Night, Samhain and Summer's End.

✦ ✦ ✦

Orange symbolizes the harvest season, and black represents darkness and the coming of winter. Thus, the two colors came to be associated with Halloween.

✦ ✦ ✦

The next time a full moon occurs on Halloween will be in 2020.

Autumnal crafts

Bring the brilliant colors of fall into your home with inspiring displays that are a treat for the eyes.

MAKE HARVEST VASES
Choose a variety of squash, including acorn and butternut, to hold seasonal bouquets. Hollow out the squash, add water and fill with blooms.

Nut wreath

֎❧💀❧֎

YOU'LL NEED ✦ **3 lb. hazelnuts in shell, or acorns with caps removed** ✦ **Towel** ✦ **Scissors** ✦ **Medium-weight cardboard, such as a cereal box** ✦ **14" extruded Styrofoam wreath form** ✦ **Newspaper** ✦ **Brown spray paint** ✦ **Hot-glue gun** ✦ **Sandpaper** ✦ **18 almonds in shell** ✦ **Gold-tone beads** ✦ **1½" head pins** ✦ **1½"- to 2"-wide ribbon, 1 yard**

1 Place nuts in a colander. Rinse. Spread out on towel to dry.

2 Cut out 3 cardboard circles, about 1½" in diameter. Set circles and wreath form on newspaper or drop cloth in a ventilated area. Apply a light coat of spray paint to cardboard circles and wreath form. Let dry.

3 Glue hazelnuts to wreath form, placing flat top of nuts against form. Cluster them as closely as possible. To ensure that wreath hangs flat against wall or door, cover only front and sides of form with nuts.

4 To make almond flowers, glue a hazelnut to center of each cardboard circle, pointy end against cardboard (if nut is too pointy to attach securely, sand until flat). Arrange 6 almonds like petals around each center nut and glue in place. Let dry, then trim any cardboard that shows between petals.

5 Glue flowers to wreath at the 5 o'clock position.

6 To add gold-tone beads, place each bead on a head pin and insert between nuts into wreath form.

7 Fold ribbon in half and loop around top of wreath to hang.

Framed leaves

∽☙∾

YOU'LL NEED
✦ **4 10" square frames
with mats and glass or
Plexiglas** ✦ **Patterned
paper** ✦ **Solid paper**
✦ **Pencil** ✦ **Scissors**
✦ **Assortment
of colorful leaves**
✦ **Glue dots**

1 Remove mat from
frame. Place mat on
a sheet of paper and
trace around outer edge
(not window). Cut out.
Repeat until you've cut
2 pieces of patterned
paper and 2 pieces of
solid paper.

2 Place mat over paper
and position a leaf
or two in window as
desired. Use a glue dot
to hold leaf in place if
needed. Reassemble
frame. Repeat three
times.

Faux pumpkins

ⓒ☠ⓒ

YOU'LL NEED (for 1 pumpkin) ✦ **4"-diameter flexible white plastic dryer duct (available at hardware stores)** ✦ **Masking tape** ✦ **Newspaper or drop cloth** ✦ **Spray paint in orange and brown** ✦ **Cardboard core from a toilet paper roll, or paper towel core, cut in half** ✦ **2 green pipe cleaners** ✦ **Fat marker or other cylindrical item of similar size**

1 Curve duct into a doughnut shape with a small hole in the middle. Join ends together with small pieces of masking tape.

2 Working over newspaper or drop cloth in a well-ventilated area, spray-paint dryer duct orange, following manufacturer's instructions. Spray-paint cardboard core brown, spraying a little paint on inside of cylinder. Let dry.

3 Curl pipe cleaners by rolling them around a fat marker, wooden spoon handle or other cylindrical item. Leave about ¾" of 1 end unrolled. Remove marker and loosen curl a little.

4 Crumple cardboard core so that it resembles a stem. Insert end of cardboard core into center of doughnut shape until it fits snugly. Insert curled pipe cleaners into center of doughnut shape, between dryer duct and cardboard core. Display on wooden pedestals or atop inverted bowls.

Leaf elbow patches

୶❧☠❧ଡ

YOU'LL NEED ✦ Scissors ✦ Felt ✦ Oak- or maple-leaf template (page 177) ✦ Double-sided fusible interfacing ✦ Iron ✦ Black felt-tip pen ✦ Sweater (opt for a flatter weave: patches will better adhere) ✦ Pins ✦ Embroidery thread and needle, optional

1 Cut 2 pieces of felt, each just big enough for template. Apply double-sided fusible interfacing to 1 side of each felt piece with iron, following manufacturer's instructions.

2 Cut out leaf template of choice. Place it on felt and trace around it. Repeat on other piece of felt. Cut out.

3 Put on sweater and position leaves over elbows, interfacing against sweater. Hold leaves in place with pins.

4 Iron leaf patches onto sweater, again following interfacing manufacturer's instructions.

5 Optional: To make the patches more permanent, use a running stitch to sew them to the sweater.

Pumpkin candleholders

୶❧☠❧ଡ

YOU'LL NEED ✦ Newspaper ✦ Serrated knife ✦ 5 pumpkins, each about 5" tall ✦ Large spoon or scoop ✦ 5 6"-tall, 1½"- to 2"-diameter candles

1 Spread out newspaper over work area. In top of pumpkin, carve a hole that's slightly smaller than diameter of candle. Scoop out pulp and seeds. (If hole is too small to pull out seeds, carve another hole in bottom for this purpose.) Rinse out pumpkin. Repeat for each pumpkin.

2 Insert a candle into each pumpkin. Candle should stick out of top by about 2". If candle is too short, place it on an inverted votive holder or an inverted cap from a shaving-cream can (or something similar).

Gather the ghouls

Don't leave your favorite friends and fiends all dressed up with nowhere to go on Halloween. Throw a party, with suitably spooky food and decorations.

Gather
the
ghouls

◆◆◆◆◆◆◆◆◆◆◆◆

FUEL-UP
DINNER MENU

Chicken Tortilla Soup

Confetti Cornbread

**South of the Border
Caesar Salad**

Ham and Jack Roll-Ups

Fuel up for fun

Put kids in the mood with a tasty menu and delightful decorations before sending them out to haunt the neighborhood.

Confetti Cornbread

Prep: 25 min. **Bake:** 35 min. **Yields:** 24 pieces

- 1 Tbsp. vegetable oil
- ½ red bell pepper, stemmed, seeded, cut into ¼-inch dice
- ½ green bell pepper, stemmed, seeded, cut into ¼-inch dice
- 1 4- or 4.5-oz. can chopped green chiles, drained
- 2 cups all-purpose flour
- 2 cups coarse cornmeal
- 2 Tbsp. baking powder
- 2 tsp. salt
- 1½ cups milk
- 3 large eggs, beaten
- 8 Tbsp. (1 stick) unsalted butter, melted and cooled
- 2 tsp. seeded and minced jalapeño

1 Preheat oven to 375°F. Mist a 9-by-13-inch baking pan with cooking spray.

2 Warm oil in a skillet over medium-high heat. Sauté red and green bell peppers until softened. Stir in green chiles, remove from heat and cool slightly.

3 Whisk flour, cornmeal, baking powder and salt in a bowl. Whisk milk, eggs and butter in a separate bowl until smooth. Stir milk mixture into flour mixture. Stir in bell pepper mixture and jalapeño. Pour batter into pan. Bake until a tester inserted in the center comes out clean, 30 to 35 minutes. Let cool.

PER SERVING: 148 Cal., 6g Fat (3g Sat.), 39mg Chol., 1g Fiber, 3g Pro., 20g Carb., 303mg Sod.

Chicken Tortilla Soup

Prep: 35 min. **Cook:** 1 hr. 10 min. **Stand:** 15 min. **Serves:** 8

- 4 6-inch corn tortillas
- 1 tsp. vegetable oil
- Salt and pepper
- 2 Tbsp. olive oil
- 1 onion, chopped
- 1 rib celery, chopped
- 2 carrots, chopped
- 1 small jalapeño, stemmed, seeded and minced
- 1 tsp. chili powder
- 2 Tbsp. coarse cornmeal
- 6 cups low-sodium chicken broth
- 8 bone-in, skin-on chicken parts (about 3 lb. total)
- 1 15.5-oz. can black beans, drained and rinsed
- 2 Tbsp. chopped fresh cilantro
- 2 avocados, peeled, pitted, cut into small dice
- 2 limes, quartered

1 Make tortilla strips: Preheat oven to 375°F. Stack tortillas and cut into ¼-inch strips. Toss in a bowl with vegetable oil, ½ tsp. salt and a pinch of pepper. Spread in a single layer on a large baking sheet. Bake for 10 to 12 minutes, until golden and crisp, rotating pan halfway through. (Tortillas can be prepared up to 5 days in advance.)

2 Make soup: Warm olive oil in a large pot over medium-high heat. Add onion, celery, carrots and jalapeño and cook, stirring, until softened but not browned, about 5 minutes. Sprinkle chili powder and cornmeal over vegetables and cook for 1 minute, stirring constantly. Add broth. Bring to a boil over high heat, then reduce to medium-low. Add chicken; simmer, partially covered, until chicken is cooked, about 30 minutes.

3 Transfer chicken to a work surface; let rest until cool enough to handle. Turn off heat under soup and skim off fat. Shred chicken and discard skin, bones and gristle. Return shredded chicken to pot along with beans. Cook over medium heat, stirring occasionally, for 5 minutes. Season with additional salt and pepper, if desired. (Can be made up to 2 days in advance to this point.) Add cilantro just before serving.

4 Serve soup hot, garnished with tortilla strips, avocado and lime wedges.

PER SERVING: 493 Cal., 30g Fat (7g Sat.), 108mg Chol., 8g Fiber, 34g Pro., 25g Carb., 534mg Sod.

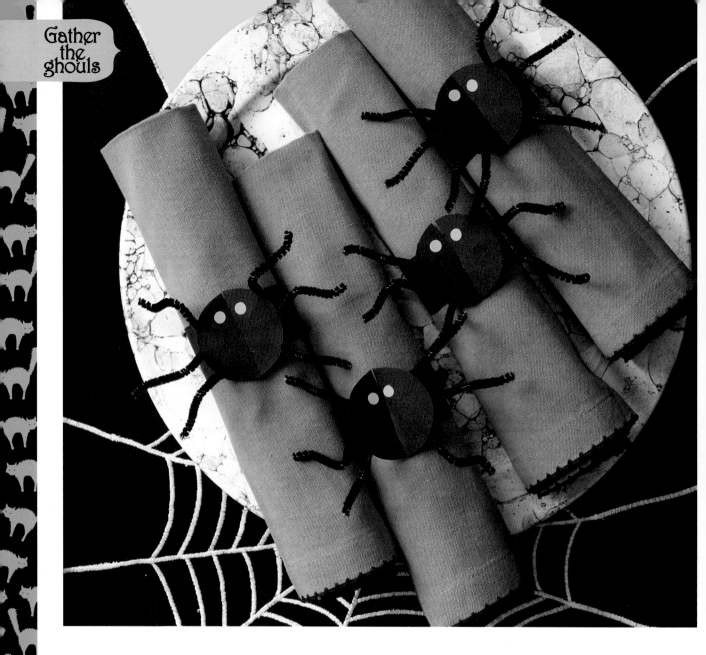

Spider napkin rings

YOU'LL NEED (for 8 napkin rings) ✦ Scissors ✦ Spider template (page 177)
✦ **4 sheets black construction paper** ✦ Pencil ✦ **16 black pipe cleaners** ✦ Ruler ✦ Tape (or hot-glue gun)
✦ **X-acto knife** ✦ Hole punch ✦ **1 sheet green paper** ✦ Craft glue or glue dots

1 Cut out template and place on black construction paper. Trace around it. Repeat for a total of 8 rings. Cut out, then cut slits following dotted line on template.

2 Cut each pipe cleaner into 3 pieces, each 4" long (6 for each spider, for a total of 48 pieces).

3 Tape 3 pipe cleaners to each half-circle on band. Start with middle leg at 3 o'clock, then tape one above at about 1:30 and one below at about 4:30. Repeat on other half-circle. Press tape on either side of each pipe cleaner to help it adhere. (If you prefer, you can use a hot-glue gun for this step.)

4 Turn band right side up and use an X-acto knife to trim any tape that is showing. If slits are taped over, use blade to reopen.

5 For eyes, use a hole punch to make 16 dots out of green paper. Glue one eye to each half-circle with a tiny dab of glue or a glue dot.

6 Bend each leg 3 times: upward near body of spider, downward at knee and upward at ankle.

7 Wrap each band around a napkin and slide the 2 slits into each other. Secure with a dab of craft glue or glue dots.

South of the Border Caesar Salad

Prep: 15 min. **Serves:** 8

෨◦💀◦൦

+ **2 cloves garlic, coarsely chopped**
+ **1 Tbsp. seeded and chopped canned chipotle chiles in adobo sauce (1 to 2 chiles), plus 1 tsp. adobo sauce**
+ **2 Tbsp. lime juice**
+ **2 Tbsp. mayonnaise**
+ **½ cup olive oil**
+ **¼ cup grated Parmesan**
+ **¼ tsp. salt**
+ **¼ tsp. pepper**
+ **2 large heads romaine lettuce, trimmed, cut crosswise into 1-inch strips**
+ **2 Tbsp. chopped fresh cilantro**
+ **2 cups tortilla chips, coarsely crushed**

1 Combine garlic, chiles, adobo sauce, lime juice and mayonnaise in the bowl of a food processor and process until smooth. With blades in motion, slowly pour in olive oil. Pulse in Parmesan, salt and pepper. (Makes about ¾ cup dressing. Can be made up to 3 days in advance. Cover and chill until ready to use.)

2 Just before serving, toss lettuce with dressing, cilantro and crushed tortilla chips. Garnish salad with additional chips if desired.

PER SERVING: 220 Cal., 19g Fat (3g Sat.), 5mg Chol., 4g Fiber, 4g Pro., 10g Carb., 194mg Sod.

Ham and Jack Roll-Ups

Prep: 10 min. **Yields:** 16 rolls

෨◦💀◦൦

+ **2 medium zucchini**
+ **4 slices packaged deli ham**
+ **4 thin slices Monterey Jack cheese**
+ **Pepper**

1 Trim ends of zucchini and discard. Using a vegetable peeler, slice zucchini lengthwise into 16 paper-thin slices; place in a single layer on a work surface. (Discard first slice of peel and seedy center.) Wrap and chill remaining zucchini for another use.

2 Stack ham slices and cut into 4 long strips. Repeat with cheese slices.

3 Sprinkle zucchini slices with pepper. Lay a ham strip in center of a zucchini slice and top with a cheese strip. Starting at one end of zucchini strip, roll it into a tight spiral; secure with a toothpick. Repeat.

PER SERVING: 51 Cal., 4g Fat (2g Sat.), 13mg Chol., 0g Fiber, 3g Pro., 1g Carb., 127mg Sod.

SERVE YOURSELF

TRY CRAFTY NEW WAYS TO MAKE CANDY TREATS EVEN MORE TEMPTING.

WHAT IS CANDY CORN?

Invented in the 1880s, the little pellets are made of mellowcreme, a concoction of sugar, corn syrup, honey and wax.

1. Bat flurry

✦✦✦✦✦✦✦✦✦✦✦✦✦✦✦✦

YOU'LL NEED
✦ Scissors ✦ Bat template (page 178) ✦ Black construction paper ✦ Pencil ✦ ¼" hole punch ✦ White construction paper ✦ Glue ✦ Mini cupcake liners, black ✦ Floral stem wire

1 Cut out bat template with scissors. Place template on black construction paper, trace with pencil and cut out. Repeat until you have the number of bats you want.

2 To make eyes, punch holes in white paper. Glue 2 circles to each bat.

3 To make wings, cut bottoms out of black mini cupcake liners. Cut ruffled liner sides into approximately 1¼" segments. Flatten out slightly. Position 2 wings on back of each bat. Attach wings with glue.

4 Punch holes in black construction paper. Position a floral stem wire on back of bat, add a dot of glue on wire, then place a black circle over glue so that wire is sandwiched between bat body and black circle. Repeat for each bat.

2. Tombstone goody bags

◆◆◆◆◆◆◆◆◆◆◆◆◆◆◆◆◆

YOU'LL NEED ✦ Pencil ✦ Small black paper bags (available at craft stores such as Michaels) ✦ Paper or thin cardboard for template ✦ Scissors ✦ Ruler ✦ Silver or white paint pen

1 To create template, trace around bag on paper. Cut out shape.

2 Draw a tombstone outline within template, leaving sides and bottom as they are while creating a decorative shape at top edge.

3 Once you've drawn a design that pleases you, fold template in half vertically and cut out drawn shape. (This step ensures that your design is symmetrical.) You may want to make 2 or 3 templates so you have a variety of bags.

4 Place template on a bag and trace around it. Cut out tombstone shape.

5 Using a ruler to center lettering, write *R.I.P.* and a guest's name on front of bag. Repeat steps 4 and 5 for each bag.

3. Pumpkin bowl

✦✦✦✦✦✦✦✦✦✦✦✦✦✦✦✦

YOU'LL NEED ✦ Sharp serrated knife ✦ Pumpkin, at least 10" tall and 11" in diameter ✦ 8" cake pan without a lip ✦ Pencil ✦ Large spoon or ice cream scoop ✦ Terra-cotta pot or glass jar, approximately 6" tall ✦ Tap light ✦ Candy corn or other candy

1 Cut stem off pumpkin. Center inverted cake pan over top of pumpkin. Trace around cake pan with pencil; using this line as a guide, cut top off pumpkin in a scallop design. (Opening should allow cake pan to fit in snugly, so make it slightly smaller than outline of pan and then carefully cut away extra if necessary.)

2 Scoop seeds and pulp out of pumpkin with spoon. Draw face on pumpkin, positioning eyes at least 2" below scalloped edge so cake pan does not show through jack-o'-lantern's eyes. Carve face. Let pumpkin dry overnight.

3 Place inverted terra-cotta pot or jar inside jack-o'-lantern at center of base. Turn on tap light and position it between pot or jar and front wall of pumpkin so that light shines through face. Balance cake pan, right side up, on top of pot. Fill pan with candy.

Have a grand vampire party

Creepy crafts! Fang-tastic food! Give 'em a thrill on the spookiest night of the year.

Sinister centerpiece

෩ ☠ ෩

YOU'LL NEED ✦ Painter's tape ✦ Spray primer ✦ Framed mirror in a size to fit center of your dining table ✦ 4 to 6 candlesticks ✦ Assortment of real or artificial fruit ✦ Matte black spray paint ✦ Bowl, preferably footed or with pedestal ✦ "Bleeding" taper candles ✦ Scissors ✦ Artificial flowers in black

1 Use painter's tape to mask mirror glass.

2 In a well-ventilated space, spray mirror frame, candlesticks and fruit with primer. Let dry, following manufacturer's instructions.

3 Spray objects with black paint. Let dry. Remove painter's tape.

4 Position mirror on table. Place bowl on center of mirror and arrange fruit in bowl. Put taper candles in candlesticks, cut flowers from stems and arrange blooms on mirror.

♦♦♦♦♦♦♦♦♦♦♦♦♦♦
VAMPIRE DINNER MENU
Spicy Popcorn

Roasted-Garlic Soup

Green Salad with Beet Vinaigrette

Sirloin Tip Roast with Carrots and Baby Red Potatoes

Green Salad with Beet Vinaigrette

Prep: 10 min. Serves: 8

✧☠✧

- ✦ 2 Tbsp. red wine vinegar
- ✦ 1 Tbsp. lemon juice
- ✦ 1 tsp. Dijon mustard
- ✦ 1 small shallot, minced (about 1 Tbsp.)
- ✦ 1 cup chopped canned or roasted beets
- ✦ ¼ cup vegetable oil
- ✦ ¼ cup olive oil
- ✦ Salt and pepper
- ✦ 12 cups assorted greens, such as Boston, romaine and red- and green-leaf lettuces, arugula and radicchio, torn

1 Combine vinegar, lemon juice, mustard, shallot and beets in a blender. With blades in motion, slowly add both oils. Blend until thick and creamy. Season with salt and pepper.

2 Pour half of dressing into a large salad bowl and pile lettuce on top. Toss just before serving and pass remaining dressing separately.

PER SERVING: 140 Cal., 14g Fat (1g Sat.), 0mg Chol., 1g Fiber, 1g Pro., 4g Carb., 81mg Sod.

Roasted-Garlic Soup

Prep: 15 min. Cook: 1 hr. Serves: 8

✧☠✧

- ✦ 4 whole heads of garlic
- ✦ 3 Tbsp. olive oil
- ✦ 6 Tbsp. unsalted butter
- ✦ 2 medium onions, chopped
- ✦ Salt and pepper
- ✦ 2 Tbsp. chopped fresh thyme
- ✦ ¼ cup all-purpose flour
- ✦ 8 cups low-sodium chicken broth
- ✦ 1 cup heavy cream, warmed
- ✦ 2 Tbsp. chopped fresh parsley
- ✦ Croutons, optional

1 Preheat oven to 375°F. Line a small baking sheet with foil. Use a sharp knife to cut ¼ inch off top of each garlic head. Place garlic cut side up on baking sheet. Drizzle olive oil on top. Roast until softened, about 45 minutes. When cool enough to handle, squeeze soft cooked pulp from each clove into a small bowl.

2 Melt butter in a large pot over medium-high heat. Add onions and 1 tsp. each salt and pepper and sauté until onions have softened, about 4 minutes. Stir in thyme and reserved garlic. Sprinkle in flour. Cook for about 1 minute, stirring, to incorporate flour. Pour in broth, increase heat to high and bring to a boil. Boil rapidly, stirring often, until slightly thickened, about 10 minutes. Let cool slightly.

3 Working in batches, puree soup in a blender. Return to pot and bring to a simmer over medium heat. Add cream, season with salt and pepper and sprinkle with parsley. Top with croutons, if desired.

PER SERVING: 290 Cal., 25g Fat (13g Sat.), 64mg Chol., 1g Fiber, 6g Pro., 20g Carb., 862mg Sod.

Batty invitations

ᑐᑐ💀ᑐᑐ

YOU'LL NEED (for 8 invitations) ✦ Scissors ✦ Bat body and wing templates (page 178) ✦ Pencil and eraser ✦ 8 sheets black paper ✦ Darning needle ✦ 16 small black brads ✦ Silver or white fine-point marker or pen ✦ 8 black envelopes

1 Cut out templates and place on black paper. Trace around them with a pencil; cut out. Use eraser to remove any remaining pencil marks.

2 Position wings on body at each bat's "shoulder" height. Experiment with sweeping wings open and closed to make sure you positioned them correctly. Use darning needle to pierce a hole through wing and body, then push a brad through both holes, attaching wing to body. Repeat with second wing. Repeat this step for all remaining bats.

3 Use marker to write message on each bat's body. Fold wings shut, then place in envelope. Address envelope with same marker.

OFFER GUESTS A BITE

Apply two dabs of fake blood to the side of your neck to mimic vampire bite marks. Can't find fake blood? Use lipstick or whatever you have in your makeup kit to create the bites instead. For guests who prefer to keep bloodsuckers at bay, make garlic pendants. Thread a darning needle with red, black or white ribbon. Poke needle through the top of a head of garlic and string ribbon through hole. Tie ends together.

Spicy Popcorn

Prep: 5 min. **Cook:** 10 min.
Serves: 8

✎☠✎

+ **1 tsp. chili powder**
+ **¼ tsp. paprika**
+ **¼ tsp. salt**
+ **2 Tbsp. vegetable oil**
+ **1 cup popping corn**
+ **2 Tbsp. unsalted butter, melted**

1 Combine chili powder, paprika and salt in a small bowl. In a large covered pot over medium-high heat, warm oil. Add a few kernels of corn and shake until they pop. Add rest of kernels, cover and cook, shaking pot often, until 4 to 5 seconds elapse between pops. Remove from heat and continue shaking pot until popping stops. (Cooking times vary; watch pot carefully in order to prevent scorching.)

2 Immediately pour popped corn into a large bowl and toss with melted butter. Place spice mixture in a small sieve and sift over buttered popcorn. Toss and serve.

PER SERVING: 181 Cal., 8g Fat (3g Sat.), 8mg Chol., 5g Fiber, 4g Pro., 25g Carb., 79mg Sod.

FRIGHT FEST
Show movies such as *Dracula, Interview with the Vampire, Fright Night* or anything from the *Twilight* series. Keep the TV muted during the party.

Lend a hand

✎☠✎

Give guests goose bumps by adding an icy hand to the punch. Fill a kitchen glove with water and knot to secure. Freeze at least 6 hours, then carefully cut glove away from ice with small scissors. Just before serving punch, float hand in bowl.

Sirloin Tip Roast with Carrots and Baby Red Potatoes

Prep: 15 min. **Cook:** 2 hr. **Serves:** 10

∽☠∾

- ✦ **1 sirloin tip roast (3½ to 4 lb.)**
- ✦ **Salt and pepper**
- ✦ **2 Tbsp. all-purpose flour**
- ✦ **2 Tbsp. unsalted butter**
- ✦ **2 Tbsp. vegetable oil**
- ✦ **2 lb. carrots (about 8 large), cut into large pieces**
- ✦ **24 whole small baby red potatoes (about 2 lb.), scrubbed**

1 Preheat oven to 325°F. Pat roast dry; season all over with salt and pepper. Sprinkle flour over roast; use hands to pat it evenly over meat.

2 Melt butter and 1 Tbsp. oil in a large roasting pan over medium-high heat on top of stove. Add roast and cook, turning with tongs, until browned on all sides, about 15 minutes total.

3 Place carrots and potatoes in a large bowl and toss them with remaining 1 Tbsp. oil. Place vegetables in roasting pan all around roast. Roast, stirring vegetables often, until a meat thermometer inserted into thickest part of meat registers 140°F for medium rare,

1 hour 30 minutes to 1 hour 45 minutes.

4 Transfer roast to a cutting board, tent loosely with foil and let rest for 10 minutes. Stick a sharp paring knife into carrots and potatoes to make sure they're easily pierced. If they're not, return roasting pan with vegetables to oven to continue cooking while meat rests.

5 Thinly slice roast and serve warm with carrots and potatoes.

PER SERVING: 533 Cal., 25g Fat (10g Sat.), 146mg Chol., 4g Fiber, 49g Pro., 24g Carb., 236mg Sod.

Bat mobile

❧ 💀 ❧

YOU'LL NEED ✦ Embroidery hoop, any size (or make a trio in 8", 10" and 14" diameters) ✦ Matte black spray paint ✦ Bat template (page 179) ✦ Copy machine ✦ Scissors ✦ Pencil and eraser ✦ Black paper, 10 to 12 sheets ✦ Darning needle ✦ Heavyweight black thread ✦ ¼"-wide black ribbon

1 Separate rings of embroidery hoop. Working in a well-ventilated space, spray-paint rings black. Make thin, even layers. Once dry, reassemble hoop.

2 Use a copy machine to enlarge bat template to a variety of sizes, ranging from 4" to 10" wide. Cut out templates. Trace bat shapes onto black paper, making about 6 bats per mobile.

3 Cut out bats. Erase any stray pencil marks from bats.

4 Pierce top center of each bat's head with darning needle.

5 Cut lengths of thread and tie each bat to a thread. Position bats evenly around circumference of hoop. Tie bats to hoop at varying lengths and secure with double knots.

6 Cut 3 pieces of black ribbon to the same length and tie to embroidery hoop at even intervals. Tie all ribbon ends together to make a hanger.

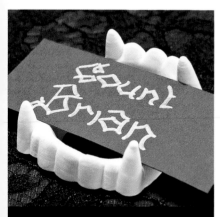

PLEASE BE SEATED
Use plastic fangs (available at party supply stores) as place card holders. Write guests' names in Gothic lettering.

Pillowcase slipcovers

❧ 💀 ❧

YOU'LL NEED ✦ Computer and printer ✦ Scissors ✦ 2 9" x 12" sheets adhesive-backed glitter craft foam ✦ Red or black pillowcases (one per chair) TIP: Use worn-out pillowcases of various colors and dye them red or black ✦ 2 to 4 yards cheesecloth (about ½ yard per chair) ✦ Double-sided tape

1 Label chairs at head of each table with your own initial (for instance, an S to indicate House of Smith). Choose a Gothic font on your computer and type the letter at a large size. Print out and cut out. Place template on back of foam sheets, reversed. Trace around and cut out.

2 Slip pillowcases over chair backs. If your chairs have arms, use scissors to cut slits in the pillowcases' side seams to accommodate them.

3 Cut cheesecloth into ½-yard lengths. Drape over and around each chair back and secure with double-sided tape, if necessary. Use fingers to poke holes in cheesecloth to give it a ragged appearance.

4 Attach foam letters to backs of chairs using double-sided tape. **TIP:** Choose chairs with tall backs for a more regal effect.

Spectacular supper

Serve up some Halloween fun with this hauntingly tasty dinner for eight.

Ghost lights

ᦂ☠ᦂ

YOU'LL NEED ✦ **24 small googly eyes** ✦ **12 white mini paper cups**
✦ **Awl** ✦ **String of white lights**

1 Glue a pair of googly eyes to side of each mini paper cup, about halfway between top and bottom and about ½" apart.

2 Using awl, punch a small hole in bottom of each cup.

3 Hang string of lights. Push 1 or 2 lights through hole in each cup.

Buttermilk-Herb Dip with Crudités

Prep: 10 min.
Chill: 3 hr.
Serves: 8

ᦂ☠ᦂ

- ✦ 1 cup plain yogurt (not fat-free)
- ✦ 1 cup reduced-fat sour cream
- ✦ 2 Tbsp. lemon juice
- ✦ ⅓ cup buttermilk
- ✦ 1 cup chopped chives
- ✦ 2 Tbsp. chopped fresh dill
- ✦ 2 Tbsp. chopped fresh parsley
- ✦ ½ tsp. salt
- ✦ ¼ tsp. cayenne pepper
- ✦ Assorted crudités such as carrots, cauliflower florets, sliced cucumbers and cherry tomatoes

In a bowl, whisk all ingredients except crudités. Cover and chill for at least 3 hours to let flavors develop. Serve with assorted crudités.

PER SERVING (DIP ONLY): 70 Cal., 4g Fat (3g Sat.), 19mg Chol., 0g Fiber, 3g Pro., 5g Carb., 185mg Sod.

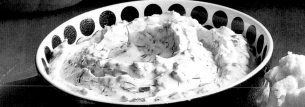

SPELL IT OUT
Use dressmaker pins to put scary words such as *eek* and *boo* on pumpkins.

SPECTACULAR DINNER MENU

Buttermilk-Herb Dip

Devils on Horseback

Green Salad

Cornbread Ghosts

Black Bean and Butternut Squash Chili

Green Salad with Celery, Walnuts and Cranberries

Prep: 10 min. Serves: 8

୧⊚୨ ☠ ⊶⊷⊶

DRESSING:
- ¼ cup apple cider
- ¼ cup cider vinegar
- 1 Tbsp. honey
- 1 Tbsp. grainy mustard
- ¼ cup olive oil
- ½ tsp. salt
- ¼ tsp. pepper

SALAD:
- 10 cups mixed greens
- 1½ cups sliced celery (about 3 ribs)
- ½ cup dried cranberries
- ½ cup walnuts, toasted

1 Make dressing: Whisk cider, vinegar, honey and mustard. Slowly whisk in oil. Add salt and pepper.

2 Make salad: Place greens, celery, cranberries and walnuts in a bowl. Toss with just enough dressing to lightly coat. Pass remaining dressing separately.

PER SERVING: 156 Cal., 12g Fat (1g Sat.), 0mg Chol., 2g Fiber, 2g Pro., 12g Carb., 188mg Sod.

Jack-o'-lantern glasses

⤳☠⤳

YOU'LL NEED ✦ **Pencil** ✦ **Scrap paper** ✦ **Scissors** ✦ **Black electrical tape** ✦ **Wineglasses**
✦ **Extra-long flexible green straws**

1 Practice drawing pumpkin faces on scrap paper to determine which ones you prefer. Small, simple shapes work best because you'll need to be able to cut them out freehand.

2 Use scissors to cut face shapes out of electrical tape.

3 Make faces by sticking cut shapes to glasses. Peel off and adjust as needed.

4 Make a green stem for each glass by knotting flexible straws. If straws are too long to fit in glasses, trim.

5 Add a stem and an orange drink to each glass. Set beverages on a tray.

Devils on Horseback

Prep: 15 min. **Cook:** 12 min. **Yields:** 24

⤳☠⤳

✦ **24 pitted prunes**
✦ **⅓ cup blue cheese, crumbled**
✦ **12 strips of bacon, cut in half crosswise**

1 Preheat broiler to high. Soak 24 toothpicks in a small bowl of water for 15 minutes. Mist a large, rimmed baking sheet with cooking spray and place a wire rack on top.

2 Halve prunes lengthwise, taking care not to cut all the way through. Place a small amount of cheese in center of each prune, in cavity left by removed pit. Wrap each prune with bacon, securing with toothpick.

3 Broil for 10 to 12 minutes, turning halfway through.

PER SERVING (1 PIECE): 67 Cal., 4g Fat (1g Sat.), 9mg Chol., 1g Fiber, 3g Pro., 6g Carb., 172mg Sod.

Black Bean and Butternut Squash Chili

Prep: 20 min. **Cook:** 6 hr. **Serves:** 8

- ¼ cup olive oil
- 3 onions, chopped
- 4 cloves garlic, minced
- 1 red bell pepper, seeded and chopped
- 1 green bell pepper, seeded and chopped
- 2 jalapeños, seeded and minced
- 4 15-oz. cans black beans, rinsed and drained
- 2 14.5-oz. cans diced fire-roasted tomatoes
- 3 Tbsp. chili powder
- 2 Tbsp. cumin
- 1 Tbsp. dried oregano
- 4 cups butternut squash (about 2 lb.), peeled, seeded and cut into ½-inch dice
- Salt and pepper

1 Warm oil in a large skillet over medium heat. Sauté onions until tender, about 3 minutes. Add garlic; sauté 1 minute. Add bell peppers and jalapeños; sauté until tender, stirring occasionally. Cook for about 3 minutes.

2 Transfer pepper mixture to slow cooker. Stir in beans, tomatoes, chili powder, cumin and oregano. Arrange squash on top. Cover and cook on low for 6 hours.

3 Season chili with salt and pepper. Serve with sour cream, salsa and other accompaniments, if desired.

PER SERVING: 276 Cal., 8g Fat (1g Sat.), 0mg Chol., 16g Fiber, 11g Pro., 50g Carb., 1,190mg Sod.

STOCK A SINISTER BAR

Soak empty wine or liquor bottles in hot water to remove labels. Let dry. Make up mysterious names for your brews and write them on white adhesive labels, adding small drawings, like a skull and crossbones. Fill bottles with water, adding a few drops of food coloring to lend an eerie tint. Seal each with a cork.

SPIDER Venom

TRANSYLVANIA TEA

TYPE O NEGATIVE extra dry

Cornbread Ghosts

Prep: 10 min.
Bake: 25 min.
Yields: 16 pieces

- **2 cups all-purpose flour**
- **2 cups cornmeal**
- **1 tsp. baking soda**
- **1 tsp. salt**
- **16 Tbsp. (2 sticks) unsalted butter, melted**
- **1⅓ cups sugar**
- **4 large eggs**
- **2 cups buttermilk**

1 Preheat oven to 375°F. Mist a large, rimmed baking sheet with cooking spray.

2 In a medium bowl, combine flour, cornmeal, baking soda and salt. In a large bowl, whisk melted butter and sugar. Whisk in eggs until well combined. Whisk in buttermilk.

3 Add dry ingredients to buttermilk mixture and stir with a wooden spoon until just combined, leaving a few lumps. Do not overmix. Pour onto baking sheet, spreading evenly, and bake until golden and until a toothpick inserted in center comes out clean, 20 to 25 minutes. Place pan on a wire rack to cool.

4 Use a 3- to 4-inch ghost-shaped cookie cutter to form cornbread ghosts.

PER SERVING (1 PIECE):
330 Cal., 13g Fat (8g Sat.), 85mg Chol., 1g Fiber, 6g Pro., 46g Carb., 261mg Sod.

Glam-slam dinner

Whip up this creative Halloween menu with a modern twist—
and put all your friends under your spell.

R.I.B.S.

R.I.B.S.

R.I.B.S.

GLAM-SLAM DINNER MENU
Bucket o' Bones
Voodoo Fondue with Apple
Mummies, Bat Bread,
Grape Eyeballs and
Blanched Brains
Polenta Pumpkins
Stake-in-the-Heart Salad
with Blue-Cheese Goo
Finger Food

Voodoo Fondue

Prep: 10 min. **Cook:** 10 min.
Serves: 8

✿◦❦◦✿

FONDUE:
✦ 1½ cups dry white wine
✦ 1 large clove garlic, crushed
✦ 6 oz. Swiss cheese, shredded
  (about 2 cups)
✦ 3 oz. Gruyère, shredded (about 1 cup)
✦ 3 oz. Monterey Jack, shredded
  (about 1 cup)
✦ 2½ Tbsp. flour
✦ 2 Tbsp. Chambord or kirsch, optional
✦ ⅛ tsp. cayenne pepper
✦ ⅛ tsp. nutmeg
✦ Salt and pepper

CREEPY DIPPERS:
✦ 2 oz. prosciutto, sliced
✦ 3 apples, cut into wedges
✦ 8 slices pumpernickel bread
✦ 1 bunch red grapes
✦ 1 bunch green grapes
✦ 1 head cauliflower

1 Make fondue: Bring wine and garlic to a boil in a medium saucepan; reduce to about 1 cup over medium heat.

2 Toss cheeses with flour. Gradually whisk into wine, 1 scant cup at a time, whisking constantly until cheese melts before adding more. Add liqueur, if using, cayenne and nutmeg; season with salt and pepper. Simmer over medium-low heat until thickened and smooth, about 2 minutes. Transfer to a warm fondue pot and keep warm.

3 Make Creepy Dippers: Wrap strips of prosciutto around apple to make Apple Mummies. Cut bat shapes out of bread and toast to make Bat Bread. Combine grapes in a bowl for Grape Eyeballs. Cut and blanch cauliflower florets to make Blanched Brains.

PER SERVING: 213 Cal., 13g Fat (8g Sat.), 46mg Chol., 0g Fiber, 12g Pro., 3g Carb., 141mg Sod.

Black dahlia centerpiece

✿◦❦◦✿

YOU'LL NEED ✦ Newspaper ✦ Black spray paint ✦ Assorted silk flowers ✦ Silver glitter ✦ Glue stick ✦ Paper plate ✦ Fake rhinestones and jewels ✦ Hot-glue gun ✦ Clear glass vase, washed and dried ✦ Masking tape ✦ Newspaper ✦ Krylon Looking Glass Mirror-Like paint

1 Go to a well-ventilated space such as a yard or garage. Cover ground with newspaper. Spray-paint flowers black. Let dry standing up or lying on newspaper.

2 Pour glitter onto plate. Dab sections of each flower with glue stick, then dip them into a plate of glitter. Attach rhinestones or fake jewels with hot-glue gun.

3 Cover outside surface of vase with masking tape and newspaper to protect it.

4 Spray interior of vase following label instructions; let dry. Remove tape and paper from outside of vase. (Inside of vase will look dull, but exterior will be reflective.) Let vase dry for 1 hour before using.

Polenta Pumpkins

Prep: 10 min. **Cook:** 15 min.
Chill: 3 hr. **Bake:** 15 min.
Serves: 8

꿈❀꿈 ☠ 꿈❀꿈

- 1¾ cups yellow cornmeal
- 5 cups low-sodium chicken broth
- 3 Tbsp. unsalted butter
- 1 15-oz. can pure pumpkin puree
- ¾ cup freshly grated Parmesan cheese
- 2 Tbsp. fresh thyme, finely chopped
- Salt and pepper
- 2 Tbsp. olive oil
- 2 or 3 scallion greens, cut into ¼-inch pieces

1 Lightly grease a large, rimmed baking sheet. In a bowl, blend cornmeal and 1 cup cold broth into a thick paste.

2 In a large saucepan, bring remaining broth and butter to a rolling boil. Whisk in puree, lower heat and return to a gentle boil. Whisk in cornmeal and cook, stirring constantly, until thick enough to hold trail of a spoon, about 5 minutes.

3 Remove polenta from heat; stir in cheese and thyme; season with salt and pepper. Stir until cheese is melted and mixture is blended. Working quickly, pour hot polenta into prepared pan and spread evenly with a spatula. Cool for 1 hour, then cover and refrigerate for at least 2 hours, until chilled through and firm. (Polenta can be made to this point up to 2 days ahead.)

4 Heat oven to 400°F. Lightly grease 2 nonstick baking sheets. Brush top of polenta with olive oil. Cut out 2- to 2½-inch shapes with a pumpkin cookie cutter. Use a spatula to transfer polenta to baking sheets. Bake until lightly browned, about 15 minutes, rotating pans halfway through. Arrange cooked polenta shapes on a serving platter. Add a piece of scallion to each, for stem. Serve warm.

PER SERVING: 253 Cal., 14g Fat (4g Sat.), 20mg Chol., 4g Fiber, 8g Pro., 26g Carb., 196mg Sod.

◆◆◆◆◆◆◆◆◆◆◆◆

CRITTER-COVERED PLATTER

YOU'LL NEED ✦ Rubber creatures in various sizes ✦ Newspaper ✦ Silver spray paint ✦ Glue stick ✦ Paper plate ✦ Silver glitter ✦ Oval or rectangular mirror, 20" long with a silver frame

1 Spread creatures on newspapers in a well-ventilated area. Spray-paint them silver and let dry. Once dry, turn them over and repeat.

2 Dab painted critters all over with glue stick and dip them into a plate of silver glitter. Once dry, arrange them randomly around frame of mirror.

'Just batty' name tags

✲✲✲❀✲✲✲

YOU'LL NEED ✦ Black oven-dry modeling clay, such as Sculpey ✦ Waxed paper ✦ Rolling pin ✦ Bat cookie cutter ✦ Baking sheet ✦ Wooden skewer ✦ Small rhinestones ✦ Silver marker or pen ✦ Ribbon

1 Preheat oven to 275°F. Knead a small piece of clay (2" x 2" x ½") into a ball; place between sheets of waxed paper and, with rolling pin, roll it out to about ¼" thickness. Cut out bat shape with cookie cutter. Repeat for each bat.

2 Place bats on baking sheet. Using wooden skewer, make a hole in each bat at the top of a wing. Press 2 small rhinestones into each bat head for eyes.

3 Bake, according to package directions; do not overbake. Remove from oven; let cool and harden.

4 On each bat, write a guest's name with silver pen. Cut ribbon; feed through hole. Position a bat atop each napkin and tie ribbon around it.

Bucket o' Bones

Prep: 15 min. **Marinate:** 1 hr. **Cook:** 2 hr. 15 min.
Serves: 8

✲✲✲❀✲✲✲

- ✦ **2 cups ketchup**
- ✦ **1⅓ cups pure maple syrup**
- ✦ **1 7-oz. can chipotle chiles in adobo sauce, chiles minced and sauce reserved**
- ✦ **½ cup dark soy sauce**
- ✦ **½ cup cider vinegar**
- ✦ **6 Tbsp. molasses**
- ✦ **2 Tbsp. ground coriander**
- ✦ **1 Tbsp. grated orange peel**
- ✦ **16 cloves garlic, minced**
- ✦ **2 racks pork spare ribs (6 to 7 lb.) or 4 to 5 racks pork baby back ribs (6 lb.)**

1 Place all ingredients except ribs in a bowl and mix to combine. Line a large, shallow baking pan with heavy-duty foil.

2 Pat ribs dry; arrange meaty side up in pan so racks don't touch. Rub on marinade; set aside 2 cups for basting. Refrigerate, covered, for 1 hour or overnight.

3 Set rack in middle of oven; preheat oven to 350°F. Cook ribs, covered, for 1 hour and 15 minutes. Uncover, turn over and baste generously with reserved sauce. Bake, basting with sauce and pan juices every 10 minutes. Turn over again after 20 minutes and cook for 20 minutes more. Baste thoroughly once more and bake for 20 minutes, until glazed and browned. Remove from oven and let stand for 10 minutes; slice. Serve in a small pail.

PER SERVING: 597 Cal., 40g Fat (15g Sat.), 161mg Chol., 1g Fiber, 40g Pro., 17g Carb., 595mg Sod.

Spiderweb tablecloth

୨୬ 💀 ୨୬

YOU'LL NEED
+ Silver glitter glue
+ 2" plastic spiders
+ Ruler + Scissors
+ 1½"-wide silver ribbon + Hot-glue gun + Plain round tablecloth

1 Note: This craft is meant for round tables. Apply silver glitter glue to each spider to add shimmer. Let dry.

2 Measure diameter of your tablecloth, then add 12" to that number. Cut 4 lengths of ribbon to that measurement.

3 Space spiders 2" to 3" apart on ribbon strips; secure spiders using hot-glue gun. Lay tablecloth on table and arrange ribbon strips on tabletop so they intersect in the center.

GET CREEPY
Use plastic spiders or bats generously! Garnish a plate with them (wash beasties in soap and water first), scatter on a table or place in guests' coat pockets.

Finger Food

Prep: 25 min. **Serves:** 8

෧ఄ☠ఄ෧

- ✦ **1 2-oz. bag sliced almonds, lightly toasted**
- ✦ **½ lb. green beans**
- ✦ **12 or 13 small carrots**
- ✦ **About 2 Tbsp. cream cheese, slightly softened**

1 Pick over almonds, selecting only whole, fingernail-shape pieces; set aside. Reserve broken pieces for another use.

2 Fill a large bowl with ice water; set aside. Bring a large pot of salted water to a boil. Trim ends of beans and blanch for 15 to 20 seconds, until they turn bright green. Using a slotted spoon, transfer beans to ice water. When cool, remove them, pat dry and set aside.

3 Peel carrots and halve lengthwise. Trim wider ends to roughly match length of beans. (Recipe can be prepared to this point up to 1 day ahead; wrap vegetables in damp paper towels and refrigerate in a sealed plastic bag.)

4 Affix an almond "fingernail" to pointed ends of carrots and beans using dabs of cream cheese. Arrange on a large platter in bunches of 5 "fingers." Serve with a bowl of sea salt or blue-cheese dip.

PER SERVING: 94 Cal., 5g Fat (1g Sat.), 4mg Chol., 4g Fiber, 3g Pro., 11g Carb., 39mg Sod.

creepy fortunes

Love lurks in creepy corners.
Watch out
for a tall, dark
and hairy stranger

Stake-in-the-Heart Salad

Prep: 20 min. **Serves:** 8

DRESSING:
✦ **1 cup mayonnaise**
✦ **1 cup sour cream or plain yogurt**
✦ **2½ Tbsp. fresh lemon juice**
✦ **2 tsp. coarsely ground black pepper**
✦ **1½ tsp. hot pepper sauce, or to taste**
✦ **1½ cups crumbled blue cheese (about 7 oz.)**

SALAD:
✦ **2 small heads iceberg lettuce**
✦ **16 wooden skewers**
✦ **2 cucumbers, cut into 16 slices (total)**
✦ **16 cherry tomatoes**
✦ **1 pumpkin, optional**

1 Whisk together first 5 ingredients. Stir in blue cheese. Refrigerate until ready to serve.

2 Cut lettuce heads in half, then quarter each half, keeping some core attached. Peel away some outer layers to make all wedges roughly the same size. Pierce each wedge with a skewer, keeping wedge close to skewer's tip. Add a cucumber slice and top with a tomato. Insert "stakes" into pumpkin (right), if desired, and serve with blue cheese dip.

PER SERVING: 381 Cal., 36g Fat (12g Sat.), 49mg Chol., 3g Fiber, 7g Pro., 10g Carb., 539mg Sod.

Sweets & treats

Delight Halloween revelers with creepy-crawler cupcakes, spiderweb cakes and dozens of other spirited desserts. These recipes taste as devilishly good as they look!

Cakes

Impress your guests with these irresistible confections, ideal for a special party.

Graveyard Cake

Prep: 1 hr. **Bake:** 35 min. **Serves:** 12

✦ 2¼ cups sifted all-purpose flour
✦ ¾ tsp. baking soda
✦ ½ tsp. salt
✦ ½ cup unsweetened cocoa
✦ ¾ cup milk
✦ 18 Tbsp. unsalted butter
✦ 1½ cups sugar
✦ 3 large eggs
✦ 2 tsp. vanilla extract
✦ ½ 9-oz. box chocolate wafer cookies
✦ 1 16-oz. can chocolate frosting
✦ 1 tube black icing
✦ 1 6-oz. bag Pepperidge Farm Milano cookies
✦ 1 7.25-oz. bag Pepperidge Farm Chessmen cookies
✦ Candy rocks, optional

1 Preheat oven to 350°F. Grease and flour a 9-by-13-inch pan.

2 Whisk together flour, baking soda and salt. In a separate bowl, mix cocoa and ⅓ cup boiling water; whisk in milk until smooth. Set aside.

3 Using an electric mixer on medium-high speed, beat butter and sugar until fluffy; scrape bowl. Beat in eggs and vanilla. Add flour and cocoa mixtures, alternating each 3 times.

4 Spread batter in prepared pan. Bake, rotating halfway through, until a toothpick inserted in center comes out clean, about 35 minutes. Let cool in pan for 1 hour. Run a knife around edge of cake and turn out onto a platter.

5 Finely crush chocolate cookies in a plastic bag with a rolling pin. Cover top and sides of cake with chocolate frosting and sprinkle with cookie crumbs. Score top of cake into 12 equal rectangles.

6 With black icing, pipe *R.I.P.* and other spooky words on Milano cookies; insert a cookie in each rectangle for gravestones. Add candy rocks, if desired.

PER SERVING: 730 Cal., 36g Fat (17g Sat.), 110mg Chol., 3g Fiber, 8g Pro., 97g Carb., 440mg Sod.

Molten Chocolate Cakes with Chunky Raspberry Sauce

Prep: 20 min. **Bake:** 12 min. **Serves:** 8

SAUCE:
✦ 2 cups fresh or thawed frozen raspberries
✦ 1 Tbsp. lemon juice
✦ 1 Tbsp. sugar

CAKES:
✦ 12 Tbsp. unsalted butter (1½ sticks), cut into small pieces
✦ 8 oz. bittersweet chocolate, finely chopped
✦ 3 large eggs, at room temperature
✦ 3 large egg yolks, at room temperature
✦ ½ cup sugar
✦ 1 tsp. vanilla extract
✦ 2 Tbsp. all-purpose flour

1 Make sauce: Place raspberries in a large bowl and stir in lemon juice and sugar. Use a fork to mash until sugar has dissolved and sauce is chunky. Cover and chill well before serving.

2 Preheat oven to 425°F. Butter 8 ¾-cup ramekins. Dust with sugar and tap out excess. Place on a large baking sheet.

3 Melt butter with chocolate in top of a double boiler over barely simmering water, stirring often. Remove from heat and let cool slightly.

4 Using an electric mixer on medium-high speed, beat eggs and egg yolks with sugar and vanilla until light and fluffy, about 6 minutes. Fold in flour and chocolate mixture. Divide batter among ramekins and bake until firm yet slightly soft in center, 10 to 12 minutes. Don't overbake.

5 Run a knife around outside of cakes to loosen and carefully turn out onto small plates. Serve warm with raspberry sauce.

PER SERVING: 451 Cal., 33g Fat (19g Sat.), 204mg Chol., 2g Fiber, 6g Pro., 34g Carb., 32mg Sod.

Spiderweb Spice Cake

Prep: 45 min.
Bake: 45 min.
Stand: 1 hr. **Serves:** 12

CAKE:

- ✦ 12 Tbsp. (1½ sticks) unsalted butter, at room temperature
- ✦ 1½ cups sugar
- ✦ 2 large eggs, at room temperature
- ✦ ½ cup sour cream
- ✦ 2 Tbsp. unsweetened Dutch-process cocoa
- ✦ 1½ tsp. baking soda
- ✦ 1 tsp. allspice
- ✦ 1 tsp. cinnamon
- ✦ 1 tsp. ground ginger
- ✦ ½ tsp. salt
- ✦ 3 apples, peeled and grated (2 cups)
- ✦ 1¾ cups all-purpose flour
- ✦ 1 cup raisins
- ✦ 1 cup coarsely chopped pecans

FROSTING:

- ✦ 16 Tbsp. (2 sticks) unsalted butter
- ✦ 1 cup packed dark brown sugar
- ✦ ¼ cup whole milk
- ✦ 2¼ cups confectioners' sugar
- ✦ 1 tsp. vanilla extract
- ✦ Orange food coloring
- ✦ 1 tube black icing
- ✦ Peanut or almond M&M's

1 Make cake: Preheat oven to 350°F. Lightly grease 2 8- or 9-inch round cake pans.

Line with parchment, grease again and dust with flour.

2 Beat butter and sugar with an electric mixer on medium-high speed until fluffy. Add eggs 1 at a time, beating well after each addition. Beat in sour cream, then cocoa, baking soda, allspice, cinnamon, ginger and salt. Reduce speed to low; beat in apples and flour until blended. Stir in raisins and pecans (batter will be thick).

3 Divide batter between pans, smoothing top. Bake until a toothpick inserted in center comes out clean, about 45 minutes. Cool on a wire rack for 10 minutes, turn out onto racks. Remove parchment; cool. Refrigerate until ready to use. (Cakes can be made a day ahead, wrapped tightly in plastic and refrigerated, or up to 3 weeks ahead and frozen.)

4 Make frosting: Melt butter over medium heat; stir in brown sugar and cook over low heat, stirring, until sugar and butter are blended, about 5 minutes.

5 Stir in milk and cook over medium heat, stirring often, just until mixture comes to a boil. Transfer to a bowl and let cool for about 1 hour.

6 Add confectioners' sugar, ½ cup at a time, whisking until smooth. Whisk in vanilla. Add drops of food coloring until icing is pumpkin-colored.

7 Place one cake layer on a serving platter. Spread approximately ¾ cup frosting evenly on top. Place second layer atop first; frost top and sides with remaining frosting.

8 Using black icing, pipe a spiderweb on top. Make spiders with M&M's, adding eyes and legs with icing.

PER SERVING: 743 Cal., 39g Fat (19g Sat.), 116mg Chol., 3g Fiber, 5g Pro., 99g Carb., 276mg Sod.

USE M&M'S TO MAKE THESE CUTE, COLORFUL SPIDERS.

Death by Chocolate

Prep: 30 min. **Bake:** 35 min. **Chill:** 6 hr. **Serves:** 12

CAKE:
- ✦ **16 Tbsp. (2 sticks) unsalted butter, cut into pieces**
- ✦ **1 lb. bittersweet chocolate, finely chopped**
- ✦ **8 large eggs, lightly beaten**

GLAZE:
- ✦ **6 oz. milk chocolate, chopped**
- ✦ **6 Tbsp. heavy cream**
- ✦ **1 can vanilla frosting**

1 Make cake: Preheat oven to 350°F. Butter an 8-inch springform pan. Wrap pan bottom in heavy-duty foil.

2 Melt butter and chocolate in a large bowl set over a pan of simmering water. Remove bowl. Stir to combine. Let mixture cool to lukewarm.

3 Whisk eggs into chocolate mixture until well combined. Scrape batter into prepared pan. Place springform pan inside a roasting pan; pour hot water into roasting pan to reach a 1-inch depth. Bake until cake is set around edges but wobbly in center, 30 to 35 minutes. Remove from roasting pan; peel off foil. Let cool on a rack. Cover with plastic. Chill for at least 6 hours and up to 3 days.

4 Make glaze: Put milk chocolate in a bowl. Bring cream just to a boil; pour into bowl. Let stand for 5 minutes; whisk until smooth. Let cool to room temperature. Remove cake to a platter; spoon on glaze. Refrigerate for up to 5 hours.

5 To create spiderweb, spoon canned vanilla frosting into a ziplock bag; snip off a tiny corner. Pipe straight lines from center of cake to outer edges. Connect lines by piping curved lines in between, creating web pattern. Pipe spider or place a candy spider on web.

PER SERVING: 464 Cal., 45g Fat (27g Sat.), 192mg Chol., 3g Fiber, 10g Pro., 21g Carb., 62mg Sod.

TIME-SAVER
If you don't have time to make edible Little Ghosts, have your kids make some out of paper and tape those to the skewers.

Pumpkin Cake with Little Ghosts

Prep: 30 min. **Bake:** 1 hr. **Serves:** 12

꧁☠︎꧂

- ✦ 2 cups sugar
- ✦ 2 cups all-purpose flour
- ✦ 2 tsp. baking powder
- ✦ 1 tsp. baking soda
- ✦ ½ tsp. salt
- ✦ ½ tsp. cinnamon
- ✦ ½ tsp. ground cloves
- ✦ ¼ tsp. allspice
- ✦ ¼ tsp. ground ginger
- ✦ 4 large eggs
- ✦ 1 15-oz. can pumpkin puree
- ✦ 1 cup vegetable oil
- ✦ 1 cup wheat-bran cereal
- ✦ 1 cup semisweet chocolate chips
- ✦ 1 cup coarsely chopped pecans
- ✦ Simple Chocolate Ganache (see recipe below, right)
- ✦ Little Ghosts (see instructions below)

1 Preheat oven to 350°F. Grease and flour a 10-inch Bundt pan. Combine first 9 ingredients. In a separate bowl, beat eggs with an electric mixer at medium speed until foamy. Add pumpkin, oil and cereal, beating until combined. Add in dry ingredients, beating lightly until moistened.

2 Stir in chocolate chips and pecans. Pour batter into prepared pan. Bake cake for 1 hour or until a toothpick stuck into center of cake comes out clean. Let cool in pan on a wire rack for 15 minutes.

3 Drizzle Simple Chocolate Ganache over top of cake. Arrange Little Ghosts around center of cake.

PER SERVING: 1,238 Cal., 64g Fat, (26g Sat.), 96mg Chol., 9g Fiber, 13g Pro., 133g Carb., 342mg Sod.

Little Ghosts

Prep: 30 min. **Stand:** 1 hr. 15 min.

- ✦ 1 24-oz. package vanilla bark coating
- ✦ 18 semisweet chocolate chips
- ✦ 5 wooden skewers (10 inches)

1 Microwave vanilla coating on high until melted, about 1½ minutes, stirring twice. Pour onto waxed paper; spread into a 16-by-8-inch rectangle. Let stand for 15 minutes.

2 Cut out 6 ghost shapes, using a lightly greased paring knife. Use chocolate chips to make eyes and mouths.

3 Remove trimmings around ghosts. Lift each ghost from waxed paper and reserve trimmings.

4 Melt reserved trimmings; spread on the back of each ghost. Attach wooden skewers and let stand for at least 1 hour.

Simple Chocolate Ganache

Prep: 2 min.
Stand: 10 min.

꧁☠︎꧂

- ✦ ½ cup whipping cream
- ✦ 1 cup semisweet chocolate chips

Microwave cream on high for 1 minute. Add chocolate chips, then stir until melted. Let stand for approximately 10 minutes before drizzling over cake.

CUPCAKE TUTORIAL

BAKE UP A BATCH, THEN TRANSFORM THEM INTO CREATURES AND CRITTERS.

MAKING EYES

Place M&M's on a sheet of waxed paper. Dab a dot of icing in the center of each. Use tweezers to place them on cupcakes.

Chocolate Cupcakes

Prep: 5 min. **Bake:** 25 min. **Yields:** 12

✦✦✦✦✦✦✦✦✦✦✦✦✦✦

- ✦ 1¾ cups all-purpose flour
- ✦ 1 cup packed light brown sugar
- ✦ ¼ cup unsweetened cocoa
- ✦ ¼ tsp. baking powder
- ✦ ¼ tsp. baking soda
- ✦ ½ tsp. salt
- ✦ 1 cup whole milk
- ✦ 1 tsp. vanilla extract
- ✦ ⅓ cup vegetable oil
- ✦ 1 large egg
- ✦ ½ cup sour cream

1 Preheat oven to 350°F. Line a 12-cup muffin pan with paper liners.

2 In a large bowl, whisk together flour, sugar, cocoa, baking powder, baking soda and salt. In a separate bowl, whisk together milk, vanilla, oil, egg and sour cream. Whisk milk mixture into flour mixture.

3 Fill muffin cups ¾ full. Bake 20 to 23 minutes. Cool on rack 10 minutes. Remove from pan to cool completely.

PER SERVING (1 PLAIN CUPCAKE): 232 Cal., 9g Fat (3g Sat.), 27mg Chol., 1g Fiber, 3g Pro., 34g Carb., 150mg Sod.

Rich Vanilla Cupcakes

Prep: 10 min. **Bake:** 25 min. **Yields:** 12

✦✦✦✦✦✦✦✦✦✦✦✦✦✦

- ✦ 1½ cups all-purpose flour
- ✦ 1 tsp. baking powder
- ✦ ¼ tsp. salt
- ✦ ½ cup whole milk
- ✦ 2 tsp. vanilla extract
- ✦ ½ cup sour cream
- ✦ 8 Tbsp. (1 stick) unsalted butter, at room temperature
- ✦ 1 cup sugar
- ✦ 2 large eggs

1 Preheat oven to 350°F. Line a 12-cup muffin pan with paper liners.

2 Mix flour, baking powder and salt. Combine milk, vanilla and sour cream. Beat butter and sugar until fluffy. Add eggs 1 at a time. Add ⅓ of flour mixture and ½ of milk mixture; repeat, ending with flour.

3 Fill muffin cups ¾ full; bake until a toothpick inserted in center of cupcake comes out clean, 20 to 25 minutes. Cool on rack for 10 minutes. Remove from pan to cool.

PER SERVING (1 PLAIN CUPCAKE): 230 Cal., 11g Fat (6g Sat.), 64mg Chol., 0g Fiber, 3g Pro., 30g Carb., 99mg Sod.

Vanilla Frosting

Prep: 10 min. **Serves:** 12

✦✦✦✦✦✦✦✦✦✦✦✦✦✦

- ✦ 8 Tbsp. (1 stick) unsalted butter
- ✦ ½ cup shortening
- ✦ 3 cups confectioners' sugar
- ✦ ½ tsp. vanilla extract
- ✦ Pinch of salt
- ✦ Assorted food coloring

1 Using an electric mixer, beat butter and shortening for about 2 minutes. Slowly beat in confectioners' sugar a little bit at a time. Beat in vanilla and salt, and continue beating for another minute until well combined.

2 Divide frosting among separate containers for each color you wish to use, then add food coloring; leave some uncolored, if desired. Frost cupcakes with an icing spatula.

PIPE LIKE A PRO
Spoon icing into a ziplock bag and squeeze toward a bottom corner. Twist bag tightly, then snip the tip off the corner. Touch cupcakes lightly with icing while gently squeezing bag.

MONSTERS BALL

RAID THE PANTRY FOR MATERIALS TO DECORATE THESE FANCIFUL CREATIONS.

STICK TOGETHER

Use small dabs of frosting as "glue"—for instance, to attach the one-eyed monster's M&M pupil to its marshmallow eye.

JACK-O'-LANTERN
FACE: mini chocolate chips
LEAF: round sour-apple candy
STEM: sour-apple straw

ONE-EYED MONSTER
EYE: large marshmallow with an
M&M and licorice for lashes TEETH:
small marshmallows cut in triangles

CREEP CURLY
HAIR: Fruity Cheerios
EYES: gum drops and licorice
MOUTH: licorice

CHOCO BAT
BODY: malted-milk ball
EYES: piped frosting
WINGS: chocolate-striped
shortbread cookie

HAIRY SCARY
TEETH: candy corn
HAIR: shredded wheat
EYES: M&M's with a dab of frosting

REST IN PEACE
TOMBSTONE: Milano cookie
(piped-on frosting letters)
ROCKS: jelly beans

BUG OUT!

THESE CANDY CRITTERS ARE SO CUTE YOU'LL WELCOME THEM IN YOUR HOME.

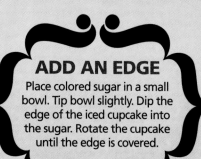

ADD AN EDGE

Place colored sugar in a small bowl. Tip bowl slightly. Dip the edge of the iced cupcake into the sugar. Rotate the cupcake until the edge is covered.

TASTY BEETLE

Use a chocolate-covered cherry for the body and a peanut M&M for the head. Attach M&M's Minis as eyes.

MS. SPIDER
BODY: Ferrero Rondnoir candy
HEAD: almond M&M
EYES: 2 M&M's Minis with icing
pupils LEGS: piped icing

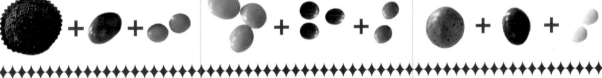

WIGGLY WORM
BODY and HEAD: 6 peanut M&M's
with M&M's Minis on top of 5
EYES: 2 M&M's Minis with icing
pupils LEGS: piped icing

MR. SPIDER
BODY: malted-milk ball
with candy shell
HEAD: almond M&M
EYES: 2 M&M's Minis with icing
pupils LEGS: piped icing

SHOO FLY
BODY: malted-milk ball HEAD:
peanut M&M EYES: 2 M&M's
Minis with piped-icing pupils
WINGS: Fruity Pasta gummy candy

CRAZY CENTIPEDE
BODY: 5 peanut M&M's with
M&M's Minis on top HEAD:
almond M&M EYES: 2 M&M's
Minis with icing pupils LEGS:
white Good and Plenty candy

LITTLE LARVA
BODY: circus peanut candy
EYES: 2 M&M's Minis with icing
pupils LEGS: piped icing

Cookies

These delightful spiders, brooms, and other sweets
are certain to disappear—like magic!

Jack-o'-Lantern Cookies

Prep: 50 min. **Bake:** 15 min. per batch **Stand:** 20 min. **Yields:** about 48

☙💀❧

COOKIES:
- 3½ cups all-purpose flour
- 1½ tsp. baking powder
- 1½ tsp. baking soda
- 1½ tsp. salt
- 2½ tsp. cinnamon
- 1¼ tsp. ground ginger
- ¾ tsp. nutmeg
- 12 Tbsp. (1½ sticks) unsalted butter
- 2¼ cups packed light brown sugar
- 2 large eggs
- 1 15-oz. can pumpkin puree
- ½ cup evaporated milk
- 1 tsp. vanilla extract
- 24 large marshmallows, halved

ICING:
- 6 oz. cream cheese
- 4 Tbsp. unsalted butter
- 4½ to 5 cups confectioners' sugar
- Orange food coloring
- 1 tube black icing
- 1 tube green icing

1 Preheat oven to 375°F. Line 2 baking sheets with parchment.

2 Make dough: Whisk together first 7 ingredients. In a separate bowl, beat butter and brown sugar until pale; beat in eggs. Mix in pumpkin, evaporated milk and vanilla. Gradually add flour mixture.

3 Put some dough in a large plastic bag; snip a corner. Pipe ½-inch-thick 2½-inch rounds onto sheets. Bake, rotating sheets halfway through, until tops spring back when touched, about 12 minutes. Top each with a half marshmallow. Bake for 1½ minutes. Transfer, on parchment, to wire racks to cool.

4 Make icing: Using an electric mixer, beat cream cheese and butter until smooth. Add confectioners' sugar a little at a time until icing is thick but spreadable. Add food coloring.

5 Gently frost cookies over marshmallow. Let frosting set for 20 minutes. Pipe icing faces and stems onto each cookie.

PER SERVING (1 COOKIE): 187 Cal., 6g Fat (3g Sat.), 24mg Chol., 1g Fiber, 2g Pro., 33g Carb., 147mg Sod.

Flying Brooms

Prep: 15 min. **Bake:** 12 min. **Yields:** 16

☙💀❧

- 8 Tbsp. (1 stick) unsalted butter, softened
- ½ cup firmly packed light brown sugar
- 1 cup all-purpose flour
- ⅛ tsp. salt
- 1 tsp. vanilla extract
- 1 package 8-inch-long pretzel rods, halved
- 2 2-oz. chocolate candy coating squares, melted
- 1 4.25-oz. tube red or orange decorator icing

1 Preheat oven to 350°F. Beat butter at medium speed with an electric mixer until creamy. Add sugar gradually, beating until blended. Beat in flour and salt. Stir in vanilla. Shape dough into 16 balls, each 1¼ inches wide.

2 Place pretzel rods on ungreased baking sheets. Press a ball of dough onto cut end of each pretzel. Press dough firmly with a fork so that it resembles broom bristles.

3 Bake for 10 to 12 minutes. Let brooms cool on baking sheets on wire racks for 2 minutes; move brooms directly to wire racks to cool completely.

4 Place brooms on waxed paper. Spoon melted candy coating over pretzel and cookie where they join. Allow to stand until firm. Decorate brooms as desired with colored icing.

PER SERVING (1 COOKIE): 196 Cal., 11g Fat (6g Sat.), 16mg Chol., 1g Fiber, 3g Pro., 24g Carb., 346mg Sod.

Chocolate-Cookie Spiders

Prep: 15 min. **Bake:** 12 min. per batch
Yields: 18

⤳☠⤲

- ✦ 1¼ cups all-purpose flour
- ✦ 6 Tbsp. unsweetened Dutch-process cocoa, sifted
- ✦ ½ tsp. baking soda
- ✦ ½ tsp. salt
- ✦ 10 Tbsp. unsalted butter, softened
- ✦ 1 cup sugar
- ✦ 1 large egg
- ✦ 1 tsp. vanilla extract
- ✦ 1 cup chocolate sprinkles
- ✦ 36 M&M's Minis or small cinnamon candies
- ✦ 72 mini pretzel sticks, about 4 inches long, each snapped in half

1 Preheat oven to 350°F. Line two baking sheets with parchment. Whisk together flour, cocoa, baking soda and salt.

2 Beat butter and sugar with an electric mixer for 3 minutes. Beat in egg and vanilla. Add flour mixture.

3 Roll a teaspoonful of dough between your palms. Roll ball in sprinkles. Repeat with remaining dough. Place 9 balls on each baking sheet, pressing lightly to flatten. Place two M&M's Minis or cinnamon candies on 1 end of each ball. Insert 4 pretzel stick halves into each side of each ball.

4 Bake 1 sheet of cookies until dry on top, about 12 minutes. Let cool on sheet on wire rack. Repeat with remaining sheet.

PER SERVING (1 COOKIE):
159 Cal., 8g Fat (5g Sat.), 29mg Chol., 1g Fiber, 2g Pro., 21g Carb., 142mg Sod.

Ogre-Eye Cookies

Prep: 35 min. **Bake:** 20 min. **Yields:** about 36

⤳☠⤲

- ✦ 8 Tbsp. (1 stick) unsalted butter, at room temperature
- ✦ ½ cup sugar
- ✦ 1 large egg yolk
- ✦ 1 tsp. vanilla extract
- ✦ 1¼ cups all-purpose flour
- ✦ ½ tsp. salt
- ✦ Green sanding sugar
- ✦ 5 long strands black licorice, cut into 1-inch lengths
- ✦ 36 white chocolate chips
- ✦ 36 brown M&M's Minis

1 Preheat oven to 350°F. Beat butter and sugar in a mixer. Mix in yolk and vanilla, then flour and salt. Roll into balls. Coat in green sugar. Bake for 12 minutes.

2 Remove from oven. Indent centers. Push licorice "eyelashes" into cookies; bake for 2 minutes. Push tip of a white chocolate chip into each center. Bake for 3 minutes. Press an M&M's Mini in center of each chip. Allow to cool.

PER SERVING (1 COOKIE): 66 Cal., 4g Fat (2g Sat.), 13mg Chol., 0g Fiber, 1g Pro., 8g Carb., 35mg Sod.

Blackberry Jam Bar Cookies

Prep: 20 min. **Bake:** 55 min. **Yields:** 24

“☠”

+ 1½ cups pecans, toasted
+ ¾ cup sugar
+ 3 cups all-purpose flour
+ 1 tsp. baking powder
+ 1 tsp. salt
+ 16 Tbsp. (2 sticks) plus 2 Tbsp. unsalted butter, cut into small pieces and chilled
+ 1 large egg plus 1 large yolk, lightly beaten
+ 1½ cups blackberry jam

1 Preheat oven to 350°F. Line a 9-by-13-inch baking pan with foil, leaving a 2-inch overhang on both long sides. Mist foil with cooking spray. Pulse pecans and sugar in a food processor until finely ground. Pulse in flour, baking powder and salt. Pulse in 16 Tbsp. butter until mixture resembles coarse meal. Transfer half of mixture to a bowl, cover and chill. Pulse egg and yolk with mixture in processor until dough forms a ball. Press dough into a thin, even layer in baking pan. Bake until lightly browned around edges and set in center, 20 minutes. Let cool.

2 Using your fingers, work remaining 2 Tbsp. butter into reserved crumble mixture. Spread jam evenly over crust. Spread crumble mixture over jam. Bake until top is golden, 30 to 35 minutes. Let cool on a rack for at least 1 hour. Lift bars from pan and place on a rack to cool completely. Peel off foil and cut into 24 bars.

PER SERVING (1 COOKIE): 260 Cal., 14g Fat (6g Sat.), 41mg Chol., 1g Fiber, 3g Pro., 32g Carb., 114mg Sod.

TAKE A SHORTCUT

SAVE TIME IN THE KITCHEN BY USING STORE-BOUGHT ITEMS.

1

2

3

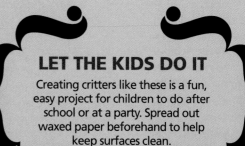

LET THE KIDS DO IT

Creating critters like these is a fun, easy project for children to do after school or at a party. Spread out waxed paper beforehand to help keep surfaces clean.

1. Witchy Cookies

Prep: 35 min. **Chill:** 1 hr. 45 min. **Bake:** 10 min. **Yields:** 15

✦✦✦✦✦✦✦✦✦✦✦✦✦✦✦✦✦

- ✦ 1 18-oz. roll refrigerated sugar-cookie dough
- ✦ Green food coloring
- ✦ 2 Tbsp. unsweetened cocoa
- ✦ 1 tube brown icing
- ✦ 20 green M&M's Minis

1 Divide dough in half. Color ½ with green food coloring.

Knead until desired shade. Place in plastic wrap; roll into a 2-inch cylinder. Freeze until cold, about 1½ hours. Knead other half with cocoa, flatten into a disk, wrap in plastic and chill thoroughly.

2 Unwrap green dough. Slice into rounds ⅛ inch thick. Space 2 inches apart on 2 cookie sheets. Roll chocolate dough between plastic wrap to ⅛-inch thickness. Using a knife, cut triangles for hats (freeze dough for a few minutes if it's too soft). Force chocolate scraps through a garlic press to make hair; place strands on sides of faces. Put a triangle on top for hat. Freeze until chilled, about 15 minutes.

3 Preheat oven to 350°F. Bake cookies right out of freezer for 10 minutes, rotating sheets halfway through. Let cool on sheets. Pipe on brown icing eyes. Add an icing dot; affix candy to it for a nose.

PER SERVING (1 COOKIE): 180 Cal., 8g Fat (2g Sat.), 10mg Chol., 1g Fiber, 2g Pro., 25g Carb., 151mg Sod.

2. Colorful critters

✦✦✦✦✦✦✦✦✦✦✦✦✦✦✦✦✦

YOU'LL NEED
- ✦ Chocolate and vanilla icing ✦ Assorted candy such as candy corn, M&M's (regular and Minis), Mentos and Fruit Roll-Ups ✦ Chocolate-covered snack cakes such as swiss rolls

1 Use icing to attach candies to cakes. Attach M&M's to cake bottoms for feet. (Mike and Ike candies and jelly beans also work well.)

2 Stick M&M's Minis to critters' backs. Make horns with candy corn and eyes with M&M's or Mentos. Pipe or attach M&M's Minis to make pupils.

3 Cut Fruit Roll-Up into tongue shapes; attach to cakes. Pipe teeth.

GET CREATIVE
Use different shapes of cakes for different creatures. For a spider, use a round chocolate-covered cake with pretzel sticks as legs. Add M&M's as eyes.

3. Witch hats and broomsticks

✦✦✦✦✦✦✦✦✦✦✦✦✦✦✦✦✦

YOU'LL NEED ✦ Green and orange icing ✦ Chocolate kisses ✦ Chocolate cookies such as Nabisco Famous chocolate wafers ✦ Yellow fruit-slice candies or spice drops ✦ Sugar ✦ Chocolate-covered cookie sticks such as Oreo Fun Stix ✦ Red Fruit Roll-Ups

1 Assemble hats: Use a dot of icing to attach a chocolate kiss to center of each cookie.

2 Decorate hats by piping orange or green icing in short spikes or simple bows around base of kiss. Or, draw a circle around kiss with piped lines of icing.

3 Assemble brooms: Flatten fruit slices in a small pile of sugar to make 2½" triangles. With a paring knife, fringe one long edge of each fruit slice, about ⅛" apart, to make bristles. Use a dot of icing to secure fruit slices to cookie sticks. Spread out the fringe with your fingers.

4 Cut a thin strip of Fruit Roll-Up and attach it above bristles, securing with icing if necessary.

Desserts

These special recipes are sophisticated enough for adult palates and whimsical enough to delight the whole family.

Pumpkin Cheesecake Bars

Prep: 15 min. **Bake:** 57 min. **Chill:** 3 hr. **Yields:** 12

CRUST:
✦ 20 chocolate sandwich cookies such as Oreos
✦ 2½ Tbsp. unsalted butter, melted

FILLING:
✦ 2 8-oz. packages cream cheese, at room temperature
✦ 1 cup sugar
✦ 1 cup canned pumpkin puree
✦ 3 large eggs, at room temperature
✦ 1 tsp. vanilla extract
✦ 3 Tbsp. all-purpose flour
✦ 1 tsp. pumpkin pie spice
✦ ¼ tsp. salt

1 Preheat oven to 350°F. Line an 8-inch-square pan with foil so that foil overhangs sides. Mist with cooking spray.

2 Make crust: Process cookies in food processor until ground. Pulse in butter. Press evenly into pan. Bake until firm, 10 to 12 minutes. Let cool slightly.

3 Make filling: With an electric mixer on medium speed, beat cream cheese and sugar until smooth. Beat in pumpkin, then eggs, 1 at a time. Beat in vanilla, flour, spice and salt until just combined.

4 Pour mixture into pan. Put pan on a large rimmed baking sheet; place in oven. Pour hot water into baking sheet until it's nearly filled. Bake until cake is set around edges but jiggles slightly in center, 40 to 45 minutes. Remove pan from sheet and allow to cool completely on rack. Cover with plastic wrap. Chill until firm, at least 3 hours.

PER SERVING (1 BAR): 340 Cal., 21g Fat (11g Sat.), 101mg Chol., 2g Fiber, 6g Pro., 35g Carb., 285mg Sod.

WHIP IT GOOD
Adorn the bars with dollops of whipped cream or whipped topping. Use mini chocolate chips for the ghosts' eyes

Spooky Crème Caramels

Prep: 20 min. **Cook:** 50 min. **Chill:** 8 hr. **Yields:** 8

- ✦ **2 cups sugar**
- ✦ **3 cups milk**
- ✦ **5 large eggs**
- ✦ **Pinch of salt**
- ✦ **1 tsp. vanilla extract**
- ✦ **½ cup chocolate chips**

1 Preheat oven to 350°F. In a pan mix 1½ cups sugar and ⅓ cup water. Cook over low heat until sugar dissolves. Raise heat to medium-high; cook for 15 minutes, until mixture turns deep amber. Divide caramel among 8 6-oz. ramekins.

2 Warm milk over medium heat until it simmers. Whisk eggs, salt, vanilla and ½ cup sugar in a bowl. Whisking constantly, slowly pour in hot milk. Strain, then pour mixture into ramekins over caramel.

3 Place ramekins in a large baking dish. Pour hot water in dish until it's halfway up ramekins' sides. Bake until custards are just set, about 50 minutes. Remove ramekins to a rack to cool. Cover with plastic; chill for 8 hours.

4 Melt chocolate; cool to room temperature. On a parchment-lined baking sheet, draw 8 circles as wide as ramekin bottoms. Turn parchment over. Pour chocolate into a ziplock bag; seal it and snip off a corner. In each drawn circle pipe 5 concentric circles and 8 spokes. Make 8 small spiders, if desired. Refrigerate to set.

5 Draw a knife around inside edge of ramekin; invert crème caramel onto a plate. Gently lift a web and place atop custard. Repeat with remaining custards and serve.

PER SERVING: 331 Cal., 8g Fat (4g Sat.), 145mg Chol., 0g Fiber, 7g Pro., 60g Carb., 113mg Sod.

Baked Apples with Cinnamon Ice Cream

Stand: 20 min.
Freeze: 30 min.
Prep: 15 min.
Cook: 1 hr.
Serves: 8

✦ **1 quart vanilla ice cream**
✦ **2 tsp. cinnamon**
✦ **¾ cup packed dark brown sugar**
✦ **1 cup unsweetened apple cider**
✦ **¼ tsp. salt**
✦ **½ tsp. nutmeg**
✦ **¼ tsp. ground cloves**
✦ **8 medium cooking apples, such as Golden Delicious or Granny Smith**
✦ **3 Tbsp. unsalted butter, cut into small pieces**

1 Leave ice cream at room temperature for 20 minutes to soften. Transfer to a large mixing bowl. Using an electric mixer, beat ice cream and cinnamon. Cover and return to freezer for 30 minutes.

2 Preheat oven to 350°F. Butter a large baking dish.

3 Combine sugar, cider, salt, nutmeg and cloves in a saucepan. Bring to a boil over high heat, stirring until sugar has dissolved. Reduce heat to medium. Cook for 5 minutes, then remove from heat.

4 Use a vegetable peeler to trim ½-inch band around top of each apple. Scoop out core and seeds with an apple corer, without piercing bottom. Place apples upright in pan. Drop some butter into each apple. Pour cider syrup over and around all. Bake uncovered, basting often, until apples are tender, 45 to 50 minutes. Serve with cinnamon ice cream.

PER SERVING: 465 Cal., 23g Fat (14g Sat.), 132mg Chol., 4g Fiber, 5g Pro., 62g Carb., 145mg Sod.

Candy Corn Cake Wedges

Prep: 45 min. **Bake:** 25 min. **Freeze:** 30 min. **Yields:** 12

☙❧💀❧☙

CAKE:
- ✦ ½ cup plus 2 Tbsp. all-purpose flour
- ✦ 1 tsp. baking powder
- ✦ ¼ tsp. salt
- ✦ ¼ cup milk, at room temperature
- ✦ 2 large eggs, at room temperature
- ✦ 1 tsp. vanilla extract
- ✦ 8 Tbsp. (1 stick) unsalted butter, at room temperature
- ✦ ¾ cup sugar

FROSTING:
- ✦ ¾ cup vegetable shortening
- ✦ 12 Tbsp. (1½ sticks) unsalted butter, at room temperature
- ✦ 1 tsp. vanilla extract
- ✦ 6 cups confectioners' sugar
- ✦ 6 Tbsp. milk
- ✦ Yellow and orange food coloring
- ✦ Orange sprinkles, optional

1 Make cake: Preheat oven to 350ºF. Grease a 9-inch round cake pan; line with parchment. Grease parchment. Lightly coat bottom and sides of pan with flour, knocking out excess.

2 In a bowl, whisk flour, baking powder and salt. In a separate bowl, whisk milk, eggs and vanilla. Using an electric mixer on medium-high speed, beat butter and sugar until light, about 2 minutes. Reduce mixer speed; beat in half of flour mixture. Beat in milk mixture, then remaining flour mixture. Increase mixer speed to medium-high; beat just until smooth.

3 Scrape batter into pan; smooth top. Bake until cake is light golden and starts to pull away from sides of pan, about 25 minutes. Cool in pan on wire rack for 15 minutes. Invert onto rack, peel away parchment, turn cake right side up and allow to cool completely. Cut into 12 wedges. Place wedges on a parchment-lined baking sheet; freeze for 30 minutes.

4 Make frosting: Using an electric mixer on medium speed, beat shortening, butter and vanilla. Add confectioners' sugar, 1 cup at a time, beating well after each addition. Add milk; beat until frosting is fluffy.

5 Reserve 1 cup of icing in a small bowl. Divide remaining icing between 2 medium bowls and tint 1 bowl with yellow food coloring and 1 with orange.

6 Working with 1 wedge at a time while leaving remaining wedges in freezer, frost pointed end with white icing, middle portion (top and sides) with yellow icing, and outer portion with orange icing. Repeat with remaining cake wedges and frosting. Press sprinkles on outer side of wedges, if desired. Chill until ready to serve.

PER SERVING (1 WEDGE):
569 Cal., 33g Fat (16g Sat.), 88mg Chol., 0g Fiber, 3g Pro., 68g Carb., 95mg Sod.

Treats

Grab a snack on the go. Whether you prefer salty, sweet or a little bit of both, you're sure to find something to satisfy your craving.

Skulls on Sticks

Prep: 20 min.
Yields: 8

- ✦ **1 Tbsp. vegetable oil**
- ✦ **½ cup unpopped popcorn**
- ✦ **4 Tbsp. unsalted butter**
- ✦ **⅔ cup packed light brown sugar**
- ✦ **1 10.5-oz. bag mini marshmallows**
- ✦ **Almond M&M's and candy corn**

1 Mist a bowl with cooking spray. Line a baking sheet with parchment. Warm oil in a large pot over high heat. Add popcorn and cover. Shake pot until corn stops popping. Remove from heat. Transfer popcorn to bowl.

2 Add butter, sugar and marshmallows to pot; cook over medium heat, stirring, until melted and smooth. Continue to cook, stirring, for about 5 minutes. Pour over popcorn and stir.

3 Mist hands with cooking spray. Form popcorn into 8 skulls around craft sticks. Set on parchment. With clean hands, press M&M's and candy corn into skulls to make eyes and teeth.

PER SERVING (1 SKULL): 328 Cal., 8g Fat (4g Sat.), 16mg Chol., 2g Fiber, 3g Pro., 60g Carb., 47mg Sod.

Transylvanian Truffles

Prep: 1 hr. **Chill:** 3 hr. **Yields:** 50

☙💀☙

+ **1 lb. bittersweet chocolate, finely chopped**
+ **1 cup heavy cream**
+ **¾ cup chocolate-hazelnut spread**
+ **¼ cup unsweetened cocoa, for coating truffles, optional**
+ **3 dozen miniature Halloween sugar decorations or toasted hazelnuts, optional**

1 Place chocolate in a large heatproof bowl. In a small, heavy saucepan, bring cream to a boil and pour over chocolate, whisking until melted. Cool slightly. Whisk in chocolate-hazelnut spread until combined. Let cool completely, then refrigerate until firm, at least 3 hours or overnight.

2 Scoop out a 1½-inch portion with a spoon. With your hands, quickly roll it into a ball; transfer to a rimmed baking sheet. Continue with remaining mixture. If using cocoa, roll truffles in powder to coat. Gently press a sugar decoration or toasted hazelnut into top of each truffle, if desired. Cover and refrigerate until firm.

PER SERVING (1 TRUFFLE): 87 Cal., 6g Fat (3g Sat.), 7mg Chol., 1g Fiber, 1g Pro., 8g Carb., 4mg Sod.

Sweet and Spicy Popcorn

Prep: 10 min. **Bake:** 35 min. **Serves:** 8

☙💀☙

+ **2 Tbsp. canola oil**
+ **½ cup popcorn kernels**
+ **1 cup roasted, salted pepitas (pumpkin seeds)**
+ **8 Tbsp. (1 stick) unsalted butter, cut into pieces**
+ **1 cup sugar**
+ **¼ cup light corn syrup**
+ **¼ tsp. salt**
+ **¼ tsp. cayenne pepper**

1 Preheat oven to 250°F. Mist 2 large baking sheets with cooking spray.

2 In a large, heavy-bottom pot, warm oil over medium heat. Add 3 popcorn kernels; cover until they pop. Add remaining kernels, then cover and shake pan continuously over burner until popcorn is completely popped, 2 to 4 minutes. Transfer popcorn to a large bowl, discarding any unpopped kernels. Toss pepitas in bowl with popcorn.

3 In a medium pot over medium heat, combine butter, sugar and corn syrup. Cook, stirring occasionally, until sugar has dissolved. Increase heat to medium-high and cook, stirring, until mixture turns golden brown, about 5 minutes. Remove from heat and quickly stir in salt and cayenne with a wooden spoon. Pour over popcorn mixture and toss to coat evenly.

4 Divide popcorn mixture between baking sheets. Bake for 30 minutes, stirring occasionally. Cool on baking sheets on a wire rack until stiff enough to break into small chunks.

PER SERVING: 436 Cal., 27g Fat (10g Sat.), 31mg Chol., 3g Fiber, 11g Pro., 41g Carb., 241mg Sod.

DIP AN APPLE

INDULGE IN THE ULTIMATE AUTUMNAL TREAT. THESE RECIPES LAYER ON THE GOODNESS: CARAMEL, CHOCOLATE AND YOUR CHOICE OF CANDY OR SPRINKLES.

1

2

DRESS THEM UP

To add festive touches, drizzle apples with melted dark or white chocolate and dip them in chopped nuts or colorful Halloween sprinkles.

1. Caramel Apples

Prep: 10 min. **Cook:** 20 min. **Chill:** 15 min. **Serves:** 8

✦✦✦✦✦✦✦✦✦✦✦✦✦✦

- ✦ **8 small apples, preferably Granny Smith (about 3 lb.)**
- ✦ **2 cups packed light brown sugar**
- ✦ **½ cup light corn syrup**
- ✦ **1 cup heavy cream**
- ✦ **4 Tbsp. (½ stick) unsalted butter**

1 Line a baking sheet with parchment. Stem, wash and dry apples and insert craft sticks in center of stem ends. Fill a large bowl halfway with ice cubes and water.

2 Combine sugar, corn syrup, cream and butter in a medium-size, heavy-bottom saucepan.

Cook over low heat until sugar has dissolved. Turn heat up to medium-high and cook, stirring often, until mixture reaches 255°F on a candy thermometer.

3 Set pan in bowl of ice water. Stir just until mixture starts to thicken into a dipping consistency.

Spin each apple in caramel until thoroughly coated. (If mixture becomes too thick, reheat gently for a few seconds.) Transfer to baking sheet and place in refrigerator until cooled and set.

PER SERVING: 426 Cal., 12g Fat (7g Sat.), 36mg Chol., 3g Fiber, 1g Pro., 85g Carb., 42mg Sod.

2. Candy-Coated Caramel Apples

Prep: 25 min. **Cook:** 5 min. **Serves:** 8

✦✦✦✦✦✦✦✦✦✦✦✦✦✦

- ✦ **¼ cup gummy worms**
- ✦ **¼ cup Halloween sprinkles**
- ✦ **1 1.4-oz. chocolate-covered toffee bar, crushed**
- ✦ **1 1.5-oz. bag Reese's Pieces**
- ✦ **¼ cup candy corn**
- ✦ **¼ cup small cinnamon candies**

- ✦ **8 small apples**
- ✦ **1 14-oz. bag soft caramel candies, unwrapped**
- ✦ **¼ cup heavy cream**

1 Line a baking sheet with parchment. Place candy (except caramels) in separate small bowls. Insert a craft stick into stem end of each apple.

2 In a heavy saucepan over medium-low heat, cook caramels and cream, stirring, until caramel melts. Remove from heat.

3 Hold an apple by its stick over pot. Spoon caramel mixture over

apple to coat, allowing excess to drip into pot. Press candy into caramel on apple. Place apple on prepared baking sheet. Repeat for each. Let stand for 10 minutes.

PER SERVING: 360 Cal., 11g Fat (7g Sat.), 16mg Chol., 4g Fiber, 4g Pro., 67g Carb., 160mg Sod.

Candy Apple Quickies

SHORT ON TIME? TRY THIS!

Prep: 30 min. **Stand:** 30 min. **Serves:** 8

✦✦✦✦✦✦✦✦✦✦✦✦✦✦

- ✦ **Halloween sprinkles and small candies, for decoration**
- ✦ **8 craft sticks, twigs or cinnamon sticks**
- ✦ **8 crisp apples**
- ✦ **1⅓ cups candy melts in orange and green**
- ✦ **1⅓ cups chocolate candy melts**

1 Line a baking sheet with waxed paper. Pour sprinkles and candy into small bowls. Insert a stick into stem end of each apple.

2 Place each color of candy melts in a separate microwave-safe, 2-cup measuring cup or

bowl. To melt, work with 1 cup of candy at a time and microwave cup on medium heat for 1 minute. Stir and then microwave in 15-second intervals until melted and smooth.

3 Dip each apple into melted candy, swirling until apple is fully coated,

then dip it into sprinkles (or sprinkle small candies all over apple). Place apple on baking sheet. Repeat for each. Let stand for at least 30 minutes or up to 1 day before serving.

PER SERVING: 603 Cal., 26g Fat (23g Sat.), 58mg Chol., 6g Fiber, 0g Pro., 95g Carb., 93mg Sod.

Beverages

Make any get-together more special with a festive drink. These thirst-quenchers add to the eerie fun.

Witch's Brew

∽◌☠◌∾

Activate 3 or 4 glow necklaces according to package instructions. Place all on a platter big enough to hold a clear glass punch bowl. Pour 1 33.8-oz. bottle chilled lemonade into punch bowl. Stir in enough food coloring to turn it bright green. Pour in 1 67.6-oz. bottle cold lemon-lime soda pop. Add ice cubes. Serve immediately.

PER SERVING: 156 Cal., 0g Fat (0g Sat.), 0mg Chol., 0g Fiber, 0g Pro., 40g Carb., 45mg Sod.

Ghoul-Aid Cooler

∽◌☠◌∾

Cover facial openings of a Halloween mask with duct tape. Line inside of mask with plastic wrap. Set mask in a bowl and fill mask with water; freeze overnight. Combine ½ cup each water and sugar, zest of 1 orange, 6 whole cloves and 1 cinnamon stick; bring to a boil. Remove from heat; let stand for 5 minutes. Strain and chill. Mix 1 quart cranberry juice with chilled syrup in a punch bowl. Stir in 1 25.4-oz. bottle sparkling cider and 1 33.8-oz. bottle club soda. Remove ice from mask and float it faceup in punch. Serves 8.

PER SERVING: 120 Cal., 0g Fat (0g Sat.), 0mg Chol., 0g Fiber, 0g Pro., 30g Carb., 29mg Sod.

◆◆◆◆◆◆◆◆◆◆◆◆

Bloodbath Punch

Cut 3 oranges into ½-inch wedges; freeze. (Try blood oranges!) In a large pitcher or punch bowl, mix 1 64-oz. bottle cranberry juice cocktail, 1 quart chilled orange juice, 1 cup chilled vodka, ½ cup triple sec and 3 Tbsp. fresh lime juice. Serve with frozen orange wedges. Serves 8.

PER SERVING: 324 Cal., 1g Fat (0g Sat.), 0mg Chol., 2g Fiber, 1g Pro., 60g Carb., 7mg Sod.

Candy concoctions

Whip up scary-good desserts with leftover trick-or-treat sweets. The ghouls are certain to gobble them up.

Almond Joy Brownies

Prep: 15 min. **Bake:** 35 min. **Yields:** 12

∽☠∽

- ✦ ¾ cup all-purpose flour
- ✦ ½ tsp. baking powder
- ✦ ¼ tsp. salt
- ✦ 8 Tbsp. (1 stick) unsalted butter, cut into pieces
- ✦ 2 oz. unsweetened chocolate, chopped
- ✦ 1 cup sugar
- ✦ 2 large eggs
- ✦ 1 tsp. vanilla extract

✦ **12 snack-size Almond Joy bars**

1 Preheat oven to 350°F. Line an 8-inch baking pan with foil so it overhangs on 2 sides by 1 inch. In a bowl, mix flour, baking powder and salt.

2 Melt butter and chocolate in a bowl set over a pan of simmering water. Remove bowl from heat.

3 In a separate bowl, whisk sugar and eggs. Stir in chocolate mixture and vanilla, then flour mixture. Transfer batter to pan. Set Almond Joy bars on top, pressing lightly. Bake 35 minutes. Cool on a wire rack.

PER SERVING (1 BROWNIE): 278 Cal., 16g Fat (10g Sat.), 52mg Chol., 2g Fiber, 4g Pro., 34g Carb., 98mg Sod.

Candy Cake

Prep: 15 min. **Bake:** 1 hr.
Serves: 12

∽☠∽

CAKE:
- ✦ 3½ cups all-purpose flour
- ✦ 1 Tbsp. baking powder
- ✦ ½ tsp. salt
- ✦ 2 cups finely chopped chocolate candies such as Snickers, Almond Joy or Reese's peanut butter cups
- ✦ 16 Tbsp. (2 sticks) unsalted butter, at room temperature
- ✦ 1½ cups sugar
- ✦ 4 large eggs, separated, at room temperature
- ✦ 2 tsp. vanilla extract
- ✦ 1¼ cups whole milk, at room temperature
- ✦ ¼ tsp. cream of tartar

ICING:
- ✦ 4½ oz. bittersweet chocolate, chopped
- ✦ ½ cup heavy cream

1 Make cake: Preheat oven to 350°F. Butter and flour a 10-cup nonstick Bundt pan. Sift 3 cups flour, baking powder and salt into a bowl. In a separate bowl, toss candies with remaining ½ cup flour.

2 Using an electric mixer on medium-high speed, beat butter and sugar until light, 3 minutes. Add yolks 1 at a time. Beat in vanilla. Beat in ⅓ of flour mixture, followed by ½ of milk. Repeat, ending with flour mixture. Do not overmix.

3 In a clean, dry bowl using dry beaters, beat egg whites and cream of tartar until stiff peaks form. Stir candies and ⅓ of egg whites into batter. Fold in remaining whites. Spoon batter into Bundt pan. Bake until a toothpick inserted into center of cake comes out clean, 50 to 60 minutes. Let cool on a wire rack for 10 minutes, then unmold cake.

4 Make icing: Place chocolate in a bowl. Warm cream in a pan over medium heat until just boiling. Pour over chocolate, let stand for 1 minute, then whisk until smooth. Let cool slightly. Drizzle icing on cake, allowing any excess to drip over sides.

PER SERVING: 642 Cal., 34g Fat (19g Sat.), 134mg Chol., 2g Fiber, 10g Pro., 79g Carb., 292mg Sod.

Milky Way Pudding

Prep: 10 min.
Cook: 10 min.
Chill: 2 hr.
Serves: 6

ᗱ☠ᗴ

+ ⅓ cup sugar
+ 3 Tbsp. cornstarch
+ 1 Tbsp. unsweetened cocoa
+ ⅛ tsp. salt
+ 2 cups whole milk
+ 3 large egg yolks
+ 2 Tbsp. unsalted butter, cut into small pieces
+ 2 tsp. vanilla extract
+ 2 cups chopped Milky Way Midnight bars (about 10 oz.)

1 Combine sugar, cornstarch, cocoa and salt in a pan. Slowly whisk in milk. Bring to a boil over medium-high heat, whisking often.

Boil for 1 minute.
2 Whisk yolks to blend in a large bowl. Whisking constantly, pour ½ of hot milk mixture into yolks. Whisking vigorously, pour yolk mixture back into pan. Bring back to a boil. Cook, whisking, until thickened. Remove from heat and stir in butter and vanilla. Stir 1½ cups Milky Way bars into pudding. Pour into 6 bowls or custard cups.
3 Cover with plastic wrap, pressing directly on surface of pudding. Chill until set, at least 2 hours or overnight. Before serving, sprinkle with remaining chopped Milky Ways.

PER SERVING: 387 Cal., 16g Fat (10g Sat.), 128mg Chol., 1g Fiber, 5g Pro., 53g Carb., 156mg Sod.

Chocolate–Strawberry Licorice Bites

Prep: 10 min. **Yields:** about 60 pieces

ᗱ☠ᗴ

+ 1 12-oz. bag strawberry Twizzlers
+ 1 cup semisweet chocolate chips
+ 1 Tbsp. multicolor nonpareils

1 Line a baking sheet with parchment. Cut Twizzlers into 1½-inch lengths; set on baking sheet in a single layer.
2 Place chocolate chips in a microwave-safe bowl and microwave on 50 percent power for 15 seconds. Stir and microwave for 15 seconds longer. Stir again.

Continue to cook and stir until chocolate chips are melted and smooth. (Alternatively, you can melt chips in a bowl set over a pan of simmering water.)
3 Dip a fork into chocolate and wave it back and forth over Twizzler pieces. Sprinkle with nonpareils. Let stand until chocolate has set. Store in an airtight container until ready to serve.

PER SERVING (1 PIECE): 33 Cal., 1g Fat (1g Sat.), 1mg Chol., 0g Fiber, 0g Pro., 6g Carb., 17mg Sod.

Peanut Butter Cup Pie

Stand: 15 min. **Prep:** 15 min. **Freeze:** 3 hr. **Serves:** 8

- ✦ **1 pint vanilla ice cream**
- ✦ **20 mini peanut butter cups, chilled, coarsely chopped**
- ✦ **1 9-inch prepared graham cracker–crumb pie crust**
- ✦ **¾ cup heavy cream**
- ✦ **2 Tbsp. sugar**
- ✦ **1 tsp. vanilla extract**
- ✦ **Hot fudge, optional**

1 Let ice cream stand at room temperature until slightly softened, about 15 minutes. Place ice cream and peanut butter cups in a large mixing bowl. Stir with a wooden spoon until well combined. Spread ice cream mixture in crust; smooth with back of a wooden spoon. Place pie in freezer.

2 Combine heavy cream, sugar and vanilla in a large bowl. Whip with an electric mixer on medium-high speed until cream holds soft peaks.

3 Remove pie from freezer. Smooth whipped cream over ice cream. Freeze until whipped cream is firm, then cover lightly with plastic wrap. Freeze until pie is firm, at least 3 hours and up to 1 week.

4 Let pie thaw for 5 to 10 minutes before slicing. Serve with hot fudge on side, if desired.

PER SERVING: 513 Cal., 31g Fat (14g Sat.), 45mg Chol., 2g Fiber, 8g Pro., 54g Carb., 335mg Sod.

**CHOOSE
YOUR CANDY**
Swap in another kind
of candy for the Snickers,
if you prefer. Peanut butter
cups, malted milk balls and
chocolate-covered toffee bars
work well. Drizzle with
chocolate syrup.

Snickers Cheesecake

Prep: 25 min. **Bake:** 1 hr. 5 min. **Chill:** 4 hr. **Serves:** 10

∽◦☠◦∾

CRUST:
+ **24 chocolate sandwich cookies such as Oreos**
+ **4 Tbsp. unsalted butter, melted**

FILLING:
+ **3 8-oz. packages cream cheese, at room temperature**
+ **¾ cup sugar**
+ **3 large eggs, at room temperature**
+ **2 tsp. vanilla extract**
+ **1 tsp. lemon juice**
+ **1 Tbsp. cornstarch**
+ **3 regular-size Snickers bars, cut into ¼-inch slices**
+ **¼ cup caramel sauce, optional**
+ **¼ cup chopped roasted and salted peanuts, optional**

1 Make crust: Preheat oven to 350°F. Mist a 9-inch springform pan with cooking spray. Wrap bottom and sides with 2 large foil pieces. Pulse cookies in a food processor until crushed. Pulse in butter. Press into an even layer in pan. Bake until firm, 8 to 10 minutes.

2 Make filling: Place a roasting pan holding 1 inch hot water on oven's center rack. Beat cream cheese until smooth. Add sugar; beat for 1 minute. Beat in eggs. Scrape down sides and bottom of bowl. Beat in vanilla, lemon juice and cornstarch.

3 Sprinkle Snickers over crust. Pour batter into pan; place in water bath. Bake until cake is set around edges, about 55 minutes.

4 Remove cake from roasting pan; remove foil and place on a rack to cool. Cover and chill until firm, 4 hours or up to 1 day. When ready to serve, drizzle top with caramel sauce and top with peanuts, if desired.

PER SERVING: 576 Cal., 40g Fat (21g Sat.), 152mg Chol., 1g Fiber, 10g Pro., 48g Carb., 417mg Sod.

Candy Corn Fudge

Prep: 10 min. **Cook:** 20 min. **Chill:** 2 hr.
Yields: 48 1-inch pieces

∽◦☠◦∾

+ **1 7-oz. jar marshmallow cream**
+ **1½ cups sugar**
+ **⅔ cup evaporated milk**
+ **2 Tbsp. unsalted butter**
+ **2 cups candy corn (about 12 oz.)**
+ **1 cup semisweet chocolate chips**
+ **1 cup salted peanuts, chopped**
+ **1 oz. semisweet chocolate, chopped, optional**
+ **1 oz. white chocolate, chopped, optional**

1 Line an 8-inch square pan with foil; butter foil. Combine marshmallow cream, sugar, evaporated milk and butter in a large, heavy pan. Bring mixture to a boil over medium-high heat, stirring constantly, until mixture reaches 235°F on a candy thermometer (10 to 15 minutes).

2 Remove from heat and stir in candy corn, chocolate chips and peanuts, stirring until chocolate melts. Immediately transfer to foil-lined pan and smooth top. Chill until set, about 2 hours.

3 In separate bowls over pans of simmering water, melt semisweet and white chocolate, if desired. Using forks, drizzle both types of chocolate over fudge. Cut fudge into squares.

PER SERVING (1 PIECE): 112 Cal., 3g Fat (1g Sat.), 2mg Chol., 0g Fiber, 1g Pro., 17g Carb., 51mg Sod.

Craft a disguise

**Who—or what—would you like to be this Halloween?
Be it princess or monster, there's a costume
here to help you bring your dreams to life.
And making it yourself is half the fun!**

Family circus

Start with clothes you may already have in the back of your closet. Add a few crafty elements and you're ready to make your debut under the big top!

Strong man

YOU'LL NEED ✦ White T-shirt, black pants ✦ Scissors ✦ Red fabric paint ✦ Silver paint ✦ Paintbrush ✦ ¾"-diameter wooden dowel, 3' long ✦ 2 black balloons ✦ Black tape

MUSCLE TANK TOP:

1 Cut sleeves off T-shirt. Paint horizontal red stripes on front of shirt. Let paint dry.

2 When front is dry, flip shirt over and paint stripes on back. Make sure stripes line up with those on front. Let shirt dry before wearing.

BARBELL:

1 Paint wooden dowel with silver paint so that it looks like a metal bar.

2 Blow up black balloons to medium size, and tie off each one at end. Use black tape to stick balloons to ends of dowel.

FINISH THE LOOK
Use a brown or black eyebrow pencil to darken eyebrows and draw in a devilish mustache. Slick hair back with wax or gel. Add temporary tattoos.

SEARCH
THE INTERNET
FOR CLOWN-
MAKEUP IDEAS.

Clown

YOU'LL NEED ✦ Colorful dress ✦ Striped socks
✦ Sneakers ✦ Felt ✦ Pencil ✦ Scissors ✦ Pom-poms
✦ Hot-glue gun ✦ Safety pin ✦ Newspaper ✦ Tulle
✦ White makeup ✦ Red clown nose, optional

1 Flower pin: Lightly draw flower shapes in various sizes on felt. Cut out. Stack two or three flower shapes together, graduated from large to small, and adhere all with glue. Glue a pom-pom to center. Glue safety pin to back of flower.

2 Pom-pom jewelry: Cut a strip of felt, about ¾" wide and long enough to wrap around neck or wrist with extra left over to tie. Glue pom-poms in place.

3 Hairband: Make a long strip of felt with pom-poms glued to it (see photo). Cut a piece of tulle, about 12" wide and long enough to wrap around head like a headband, with some left over to tie. Gather the tulle in your hand, then wrap pom-pom strip around it, leaving tails of tulle free for tying. Glue pom-pom strip to tulle.

Cotton-candy vendor

❧❀☙

YOU'LL NEED ✦ White shirt ✦ Black pants ✦ Sturdy box, about 14" x 9" x 6" ✦ X-acto knife ✦ Red and white acrylic paint ✦ Paintbrush ✦ Black permanent marker ✦ 6 3" x 6" Styrofoam cones ✦ White paper, 6 sheets ✦ Tape ✦ Polyester stuffing ✦ Small bucket ✦ Hot-glue gun ✦ 1¾"-wide ribbon, 4' long ✦ White poster board ✦ Stapler ✦ Pink tissue paper, optional ✦ Craft glue

1 Remove top of box, leaving bottom and 4 sides. Use an X-acto knife to cut out 6 circles from box bottom. Circles should be big enough for ⅓ of the cone to fit through hole.

2 Invert box so that bottom is facing up. Paint vertical red and white stripes along sides of box. Write COTTON CANDY, $1 on front of box with marker.

3 Cotton candy cones: Mix red and white paint to make pink. Make a dye by mixing ¼ cup pink acrylic paint with 4 cups water. Dip polyester stuffing into dye until fully saturated. Let dry. Wrap each Styrofoam cone in a piece of white paper (to elongate cone) and tape seam. Divide stuffing into 6 balls. Use hot-glue gun to adhere stuffing to cones. Place cones into holes in box top.

4 Cut a length of ribbon long enough to extend from box edges and around your neck. Box should hang just below waist. Glue ribbon to sides of box.

5 Hat: Cut a strip of poster board 6" x 24". Fold a 1" cuff along length of poster-board strip. Fold entire strip in half at 12" mark. Staple short edges together. Paint cuff red. Decorate with pink tissue paper if desired.

Ringmaster

YOU'LL NEED ✦ **Dinner plate at least 10" in diameter** ✦ **2 pieces black poster board** ✦ **Pencil** ✦ **Scissors** ✦ **Bowl that fits your head** ✦ **X-acto knife** ✦ **Stapler** ✦ **Hot-glue gun** ✦ **2 yards red fabric** ✦ **Gold ribbon** ✦ **Tape measure** ✦ **Old black suit or tuxedo jacket (to be cut up)** ✦ **Paper** ✦ **Tape** ✦ **2 yards black fabric** ✦ **White shirt** ✦ **Black bow tie** ✦ **Black pants**

TOP HAT:

1 Invert dinner plate on black poster board and trace around it; repeat. Cut out both circles. Invert bowl on 1 circle and trace around. Cut out inner circle with X-acto knife. Repeat on other circle. Save 1 of the inner-circle cutouts for later. You should have 2 doughnut shapes.

2 Cut an 11" by 13" rectangle out of black poster board. Make a 1½" fold lengthwise along top edge and another 1½" fold lengthwise along bottom edge. Cut slits at 1" intervals along both long edges to form tabs.

3 Bend rectangle into a cylinder and staple edges together. Bend bottom tabs outward at a 90-degree angle and glue between 2 doughnut shapes. Bend top tabs inward at a 90-degree angle. Take the inner circle that you set aside in the first step and use it as top of hat, applying glue to tabs.

4 Cut a strip of red fabric 2" x 13". Glue around hat where brim meets crown. Add gold ribbon as trim, gluing in place.

TAILCOAT:

1 Measure across bottom hem of jacket. This measurement will be the width of the tails. For length of tails, try on jacket and measure how long you want them to be.

2 Make a pattern: Using the 2 measurements from step 1 above, tape several pieces of paper together to form a rectangle corresponding to the desired length and width of tails. Fold rectangle in half widthwise. Draw a point at one end. Cut out. Place pattern on red fabric and trace around it. Cut out. Place pattern on black fabric and trace around it. Draw a 1" border around initial tracing. Cut out.

3 Glue red fabric to black fabric, wrong sides together. Glue gold trim along edge of red fabric. Glue straight edge of tails to inside hem of jacket.

4 Use remaining red fabric and trim to embellish cuffs, edges of pockets and lapels. Glue in place.

Scrub-a-dub-dub

Lather up in a bathtub made out of a laundry basket, with Ping-Pong-ball soap bubbles. Don't forget your rubber ducky!

Bubble bath

YOU'LL NEED ✦ **Heavy-duty scissors or box cutter** ✦ **Soft round plastic laundry basket with solid sides (not basket weave)** ✦ **1"-wide ribbon, 1 yard** ✦ **White foam core** ✦ **X-acto knife** ✦ **Warm-glue gun** ✦ **White tissue paper** ✦ **About 60 Ping-Pong balls** ✦ **Clear plastic Christmas ornaments and white balloons, optional** ✦ **Beige tights** ✦ **Swimsuit or leotard** ✦ **Shower cap**

1 Using heavy-duty scissors or a box cutter, cut a hole in bottom of laundry basket. The hole should be big enough for the wearer to step into and pull up basket to hips. For straps, cut 2 lengths of ribbon long enough to extend from inside front of basket to inside back of basket, with enough slack to fit over child's shoulders. Glue ribbons in place.

2 Invert basket on foam core and trace around. Cut out circle with X-acto knife, then cut a circle out of its middle (making a doughnut shape). Cut shape in half. The 2 halves will sit on top of basket, forming a base for bubbles.

3 Glue crumpled white tissue paper to foam core in cloudlike formations. Glue Ping-Pong balls to tissue paper. Add clear plastic ornaments and inflated white balloons if desired, gluing them to tissue paper.

4 Assemble costume: Have child put on tights and swimsuit or leotard, then step into laundry basket and pull it up to desired height. Using warm glue gun—hot glue can burn your child—affix foam core semicircle to edge of laundry basket, 1 piece in front and 1 in back. Adjust shoulder straps if needed.

KEEP IN MIND
This costume works best for kids 3' to 4' tall. If they're any bigger, the laundry basket won't fit.

Monsters, robots and rockets

Go space-age, scary or something in-between. Use your imagination to come up with ways to customize these costumes.

Little lizard

❧•☠•☙

YOU'LL NEED ✦ Stirrer stick ✦ Tablespoon ✦ Yellow poster paint ✦ Water ✦ Bowl ✦ 2½"-diameter Styrofoam ball ✦ Scissors ✦ Bubble Wrap or newspaper ✦ Wooden spoon ✦ Craft glue ✦ Needle and thread or 12 medium-size safety pins ✦ Spike templates (page 180) ✦ Marker ✦ 2 9" x 12" sheets yellow craft foam ✦ Green thermal top and pants ✦ Extra thermal top or green kneesock ✦ Yellow rain boots ✦ Yellow dishwashing gloves ✦ Yellow sunglasses or goggles ✦ Green ski mask with face opening

1 Mix 5 Tbsp. paint with 1 Tbsp. water in a bowl. Place Styrofoam ball in bowl and let it soak, turning every 10 to 15 minutes. When it attains desired shade of yellow, remove from bowl and let dry.

2 To make tail, cut cuff and sleeve off extra top (if using kneesock, cut off at ankle), and trim end into a V shape. Stuff with Bubble Wrap or newspaper, leaving 1" unstuffed at both ends.

3 Insert wooden-spoon handle about halfway through Styrofoam ball, then remove. Pour about 1" of glue into hole. Insert pointed end of tail into hole as far as possible; wipe away excess glue. Let dry.

4 Sew or pin tail to seat of thermal pants. Cut out small, medium and large spike templates and trace each onto yellow craft foam 4 times. Mark each spike with dotted line as shown on template. Separate all spikes into same-size pairs; glue each pair together from tip of triangle to dotted line.

5 Starting at end of tail, spread tabs of smallest spike apart, apply glue and adhere to tail. Follow with a medium-size spike, then a large one.

6 Attach remaining spikes to ski mask (as you did with tail); start with largest spike at forehead and work toward back of head, adding spikes in descending sizes.

Retro robot

∽◌☠◌∾

YOU'LL NEED ✦ Corrugated cardboard box as long as child's torso and several inches wider than shoulders ✦ Box cutter ✦ Pencil ✦ Silver spray paint ✦ Piece of cardboard slightly smaller than face of box ✦ 18 plain plastic buttons ✦ Red spray paint ✦ 12 flat metal buttons with shanks (6 1½", 2 2" and 4 2½") ✦ Hot-glue gun ✦ Scissors ✦ 3 11" x 17" foam sheets, 1 each in red, yellow and orange ✦ Fiskars scallop paper edger or pinking shears ✦ Printer and plain white paper ✦ Old bike helmet ✦ Aluminum foil ✦ Pipe cleaners in black and white ✦ Silver dryer-duct hose, 2 yards ✦ Silver duct tape ✦ Safety pins ✦ Gray sweat suit ✦ Red gloves ✦ Sunglasses

1 Remove box's top flaps. Hold box against child's torso and mark cutouts for neck and armholes. Cut a deep semicircle hole for neck; for legs, cut out a rectangle, leaving a 2" lip on each side. For arms, cut holes slightly wider than diameter of dryer-duct hose and twice as long.

2 In a well-ventilated area, use silver spray paint to coat box, inside and out, plus one side of cardboard piece and all plain plastic buttons. Let dry; repeat. Paint all 2" and 2½" metal buttons red. Let dry; repeat.

3 Center cardboard piece on front of box; glue in place. Cut red foam sheet to be smaller all around than cardboard piece. Center on cardboard piece; glue.

4 To make control panel, cut shapes from orange and yellow foam, using photo (above) as guide. Layer foam shapes on top of one another; glue. Trim some shapes using scallop-edge scissors or pinking shears. Glue on metal and plastic buttons, reserving some to decorate helmet.

5 Use computer and printer to make control-panel labels, such as COMPUTE and PRESS. Fold a sheet of printed text accordion-style and glue to control panel.

6 Wrap bike helmet in foil; glue foil in place. Decorate with twisted pipe cleaners and buttons.

7 Cut 2 pieces of dryer-duct hose to length of child's arm. Cover any sharp edges with layers of duct tape. Put sweat suit and box on child, then fit hose over arms. Secure to sleeves with safety pins. Finish with helmet, gloves and sunglasses.

HOW IT'S DONE
Looking at the costume from the back, it's easier to see how the box should be cut. Since it should rest on the shoulders, cut a shallow semicircle for the neck hole so the box doesn't sit too far down. The upper arm stays inside the box.

Frankenstein

❧❀❧

YOU'LL NEED ✦ Scissors ✦ Plastic gallon jug ✦ Sandpaper ✦ Paintbrush ✦ Primer ✦ Green paint ✦ Mounting tape ✦ Fake fur ✦ Hot-glue gun ✦ 2 ⅝" bolts ✦ Red puffy paint ✦ Gray or silver pipe cleaners ✦ Masking tape ✦ Black suit jacket, 2 sizes too large ✦ Purple felt ✦ Sewing needle ✦ Yellow yarn ✦ Loose pants ✦ Rope ✦ High-top sneakers ✦ Green socks ✦ T-shirt

HEADPIECE:

1 Use scissors to cut plastic jug in half horizontally. Discard top (pouring end). Invert bottom of jug on top of child's head and mark an edge line just below hairline; cut along it. Sand edges until no longer sharp. Paint jug with primer, inside and out. Let dry, then paint with green paint, inside and out.

2 For cushioning, apply 1"-long pieces of mounting tape inside jug, wherever it may rub against child's head.

3 For hair, cut a 6" x 15" rectangle of fake fur, with one of the short ends curved to look like a hairline. Turn fur wrong side up and apply glue along edges to seal.

4 Hold scissors closed and use point to make small holes on either side of jug, where temples will be. Twist scissors to widen hole until it is slightly smaller than shaft of bolt. Screw about ¼" of bolt into each hole.

5 Draw a scar across forehead from bolt to bolt using red puffy paint. Let paint dry completely.

6 Add "staples" to scar: For each one, make a pair of small holes, one above scar and one below it. Make a total of 7 pairs of holes. Cut 7 2" pieces of pipe cleaner. Insert ends of 1 piece into each pair of holes. Close staples on inside of jug, covering ends with masking tape.

7 Attach hair: Lay fur piece on center of jug, Mohawk-style, curved end at front. Use hot-glue gun to attach. Run your fingers against grain of fur to muss it up.

CLOTHES:

1 Blazer: Cut two oval elbow patches out of purple felt. Sew a patch to each elbow of jacket, using yellow yarn. Make the stitches oversize and cartoonish.

2 Pants: Cut pant legs so they hang about 2" to 3" above floor. Shred each leg, cutting or tearing 4" to 5" up leg. Fray ends of rope and thread it through belt loops. Tie ends in a knot.

3 Shoes: Remove laces and set aside. Cut off sneakers' tongues and upper portion of toes (not soles). Scuff the grommets with sandpaper. Stuff paper towels or plastic bags into toes of socks. Put socks on feet, then put feet in sneakers and re-lace. Tie laces, then cut off and fray ends.

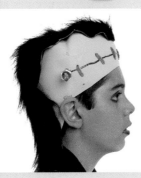

FRANK'S HEAD
A gallon milk jug, cut and inverted, forms the base of the headpiece. Fake fur is used for the hair. The scar is painted on, and the staples are made of pipe cleaners. Complete the look with a bolt on each side.

Rocket man

✆ ☠ ✆

YOU'LL NEED ✦ 2 1-liter soda bottles ✦ Silver spray paint ✦ Old bike or skateboard helmet ✦ 6" x 6" piece of cardboard ✦ Masking tape ✦ Gray sweatshirt and sweatpants ✦ Acrylic paint in silver, red and blue ✦ Paintbrush ✦ 3 bottle caps ✦ Hot-glue gun ✦ Paper plate ✦ CD (or DVD) ✦ 3 1" self-adhesive Velcro strips ✦ Scissors ✦ 2 plastic tablecloths, 1 red and 1 yellow ✦ Ruler ✦ Scotch tape ✦ Wide ribbon in red or silver (or straps cut from an old backpack or the inside of a suitcase) ✦ Gloves ✦ Silver high-top sneakers ✦ Goggles

1 Remove caps and rings from soda bottles. Spray-paint soda bottles, helmet and 6" x 6" piece of cardboard silver. Let dry.

2 Apply masking tape stripes along sweatshirt arms and pant legs.

3 For emblem: Paint bottle caps 3 different colors. Let dry. Place a pea-size blob of hot glue on a paper plate; dip bottle cap into it, then glue cap to CD. Repeat for each cap. Apply 3 1" strips of Velcro to back of CD (side without bottle caps). Pair each strip with its mate, peel off adhesive covers and press CD against sweatshirt to adhere.

4 For jet pack: Use scissors to cut 15 red and 15 yellow strips of tablecloth, each about 1" wide. Length should vary between 6" and 12". Snip 1 end of each strip into a point. Lay 15 strips down side by side on table, pointed ends facing same direction. Lay tape across blunt end of each strip; turn over and lay another piece of tape on top. Roll taped end around finger and tape together (end should look like a shoelace aglet). Repeat with remaining 15 strips. Insert 1 bunch of strips into spout of each bottle and secure with glue. Glue bottles together.

5 Attach straps to cardboard in backpack fashion: Cut small slits in cardboard and gently push straps through with a butter knife. Staple in place, then cover with masking tape for extra security.

6 Glue bottles to cardboard so that streamers are pointing downward.

IT'S IN THE BAG

Decorate large paper bags for trick-or-treating and small ones for goody bags.

TREAT THEM

Send guests home with something special. Fill goody bags with a handful of candy and add a small favor, like a decorated mini pumpkin.

Make a design

1. Stripes

Apply pieces of washi tape or patterned duct tape to bag. Or cut strips of patterned and solid paper and glue them to bag.

2. Dots

Use round adhesive stickers as dots, or use circle paper punches in different sizes to make dots out of colored paper. Glue dots to bag.

3. Shapes

Cut out cat template (page 181) to use as a stencil. Tape it to bag and fill in with glue. Place a strip of orange paper across neck as a collar. Top the rest of the glue with black glitter. Let dry.

4. Words

Stamp EEK!, BOO! or some other message on your bag using letter stamps and an ink pad.

Finish up

✦ For each goody bag, fold top of bag over several times and close with a sticker. Or cut edge into jagged points and then cinch bag with a tie made of gathered tulle.

✦ For a trick-or-treat bag that needs a handle, cut out a square from each side of bag, about 1½" from top edge. Reinforce handle by applying strips of duct tape inside bag, around edges of cutout area.

Dazzling diva

ෙ☠ෙ

YOU'LL NEED ✦ **3' x 3' piece of gold fabric** ✦ **Safety pins** ✦ **Black leggings** ✦ **Metallic ballet flats** ✦ **Gold-tone bangles** ✦ **Scissors** ✦ **Gold cardboard** ✦ **Glue** ✦ **Gold and pink glitter** ✦ **Gold-tone hoop earrings** ✦ **Cardboard jewelry gift box**

1 Dress: Tie 2 adjacent corners of fabric in a knot to create dress's halter top. Pin back of dress closed with safety pins from bottom to middle of back. (Shorten dress if needed.) Wear with leggings, ballet flats and bangles.

2 Go glam with craft jewelry and a fake cell phone. Cut 2 circles out of cardboard and decorate with glue and glitter. When dry, glue circles to hoop earrings. For phone, coat gift box with glue and roll in pink glitter.

CELEBRITY INSPIRATION
Katy Perry, Beyoncé, Selena Gomez

No~sew pop stars

Unleash your inner punk rocker, rapper or country crooner. Find the getup that embodies this supersize dream and take center stage for the night.

OLD-SCHOOL RAPPER

YOU'LL NEED ✦ **Gold cardboard** ✦ **Glue** ✦ **Gold glitter** ✦ **Hole punch** ✦ **Gold cord** ✦ **Tracksuit** ✦ **Oversize T-shirt** ✦ **Trucker cap** ✦ **Sneakers**

1 Jewelry: Decorate circles of gold cardboard with glue and glitter; let dry.

2 Punch a hole through each circle and hang from a loop of gold cord to finish each necklace. Put on clothing and all jewelry.

CELEBRITY INSPIRATION
Eminem,
Run-D.M.C.,
Kid Rock

Rock drummer

✲ 💀 ✲

YOU'LL NEED ✦ ⅜"-diameter dowel, about 3' long, cut in half ✦ Temporary tattoos ✦ Electric pencil sharpener ✦ Sandpaper ✦ Flag bandanna ✦ Oversize sleeveless T-shirt ✦ Baggy camouflage shorts ✦ Sneakers ✦ Wig, optional

1 To shape drumsticks, sharpen both pieces of dowel at one end with an electric pencil sharpener. Sand lightly to smooth all surfaces and make sharp points dull and rounded.

2 Apply tattoos. Temporary designs go on in 5 minutes and last up to 4 days if not washed off.

3 For more hair: Put on a shaggy wig, then a bandanna.

CELEBRITY INSPIRATION
Blink-182's Travis Barker, Bon Jovi's Tico Torres, Kings of Leon's Nathan Followill

Punk rocker

CELEBRITY
INSPIRATION
Siouxsie Sioux,
Miley Cyrus,
Pink

YOU'LL NEED ✦ **Baby bonnet** ✦ **Felt** ✦ **Cardboard** ✦ **Fabric glue** ✦ **Needle and thread** ✦ **Ribbon** ✦ **Self-adhesive Velcro tabs** ✦ **Tank top** ✦ **Plaid skirt** ✦ **Dog tags (on long chain, for safety)** ✦ **High-top sneakers**

1 Snip a Mohawk: Trim brim off bonnet. Cut a 2" x 8" strip of felt and make 3 2" slits, spaced ½" apart, along its length. Cut 3 cardboard triangles, each 4" high and 2" wide. Cover each with felt triangles on both sides. Insert base of each triangle into a slit in felt strip, fold over a ½" seam on bottom and glue into place. Pin strip, triangles facing up, to bonnet; whipstitch to secure.

2 Create wrist cuffs. Cut lengths of ribbon and attach Velcro to each end.

CELEBRITY
INSPIRATION
Tim McGraw,
Kenny Chesney,
Keith Urban

Country crooner

YOU'LL NEED ✦ **Plastic needlepoint grid** ✦ **Brown yarn** ✦ **Needle and thread** ✦ **T-shirt** ✦ **Felt** ✦ **Silver cardboard** ✦ **Glue** ✦ **Glitter** ✦ **Self-adhesive Velcro tab** ✦ **Cowboy hat** ✦ **Button-front shirt** ✦ **Jeans**

1 Chest hair: Cut needlepoint grid into a triangular patch and loop yarn through it; sew to front of T-shirt.

2 Belt and buckle: Cut a 1½"-wide strip of felt to use as a belt. Cut a large oval out of cardboard to serve as buckle. Glue oval to center of felt and decorate with glue and glitter; let dry. Attach self-adhesive Velcro to ends of felt strip for belt closure.

Wings and tutus

Morph into an ethereal moth, angel or ballerina with these tulle creations.

Wings

**YOU'LL NEED ✦ 1 yard tulle ✦ 2 6"
wooden tongue depressors ✦ Scissors ✦ Hot-glue gun
✦ 4" x ¾" piece of felt**

1 Keep tulle folded as it was on bolt. Cut into 2 18" pieces. Lay tulle on table, folded edge to your left and perpendicular to table edge. Starting with edge closest to you, roll tulle. Cut roll into 3"-wide segments. Unrolled, strips should be 3" x 18". Repeat for remaining piece of tulle.

2 Attach tulle to tongue depressors using loops: Fold a strip of tulle in half lengthwise. Place a tongue depressor on top of folded tulle, perpendicular to it and near fold. Wrap the 2 ends of tulle strip around tongue depressor and thread them through folded loop. Pull tight to form a knot around tongue depressor. Continue with additional strips until tongue depressor is completely full. Repeat on second tongue depressor.

3 Lay tongue depressors next to each other with tulle extending in opposite directions. Apply glue to inside edges of depressors to form a seam. Glue strip of felt over seam, centering it on depressors.

4 Braid 3 strips of tulle together and repeat, for a total of 2 braids. To make straps, trim braids so each is long enough to fit comfortably over a shoulder. Glue 1 strap to each depressor, attaching 1 end to top and 1 end to bottom of stick.

MOTH
Teased hair and pale makeup with a touch of glitter help give this moth a fairylike quality. Her dress is actually a women's-size shirt, purchased at a thrift store and cut to the right length.

Tutu

ৎৡ☠ৡৎ

**YOU'LL NEED ✦ 3 yards tulle ✦ Scissors
✦ Tape measure ✦ ¾"-wide ribbon, about 4' long**

1 Keep tulle folded as it was on bolt. Cut into 3 pieces, each 1 yard long. Lay tulle on table, folded edge perpendicular to table edge. Starting with edge closest to you and working away from you, roll tulle. Cut roll into 3"-wide segments. Unrolled, strips should measure 3" x 3'. Repeat for each 1-yard piece of tulle.

2 Cut a length of ribbon 2' longer than child's waist measurement. Knot ribbon twice, 1' from each end.

3 Attach tulle to ribbon using loops: Fold a strip of tulle in half lengthwise. Working between knots, place folded end of tulle behind ribbon. Wrap the two ends of tulle strip around ribbon and thread them through folded loop. Pull ends tight to form a knot around ribbon. Repeat until space between knots is completely covered in knots.

4 Tie tutu around waist. Trim ends of ribbon. For more fullness, make 2 tutus and layer them together.

Farm-fresh

Start with a sweat suit, then add a few flourishes. These cute costumes are deliciously fun!

Ripe tomato

YOU'LL NEED ✦ **Large safety pin** ✦ **Elastic band, 1 yard long** ✦ **Red sweat suit, plus additional red sweatshirt 2 sizes larger** ✦ **Scissors** ✦ **Sewing needle** ✦ **Thread** ✦ **4 bags fiberfill** ✦ **Leaf templates (pages 182–183)** ✦ **Rubber band** ✦ **3 9" x 12" pieces green felt** ✦ **Chalk** ✦ **Hot-glue gun**

1 Fasten safety pin to 1 end of elastic. Working on large sweatshirt, cut slit in inside of waistband and insert safety pin. Work safety pin around waistband and back out through slit. Remove pin and tie ends of elastic together so that waistband fits tightly around child's hips, creating blouson effect. Trim excess elastic.

2 Cut sleeves off large sweatshirt and set aside. Pull large sweatshirt over small sweatshirt so that small sweatshirt forms a lining. Baste bottom edge of large sweatshirt to bottom edge of small sweatshirt. Add fiberfill between sweatshirts until large one is taut. Baste armholes and neck band of large sweatshirt to small sweatshirt.

3 Cut out leaf templates for hat and neck band. Stack 2 pieces of felt, then lay neck-band template on top and trace; cut out. Sew pieces together to form an oval.

4 For hat, take 1 sleeve from large sweatshirt and turn inside out. Cut off cuff. Gather narrow end together with a rubber band. Turn sleeve right-side out and cut down to fit child's head.

5 Lay leaf template for hat atop green felt and trace; cut out. Stitch leaf to top of hat.

Bunch of grapes

❧ 💀 ❧

YOU'LL NEED ✦ Dessert plate ✦ Two shades
of purple cotton fabric, 1 yard each ✦ Chalk
✦ Scissors ✦ Sewing needle ✦ Thread ✦ Two bags
fiberfill ✦ Purple sweatshirt ✦ Grape-leaf
template (page 184) ✦ Copier and plain white paper
✦ 3 9" x 12" pieces green felt ✦ Green medium-point
felt-tip marker ✦ Hot-glue gun ✦ Additional purple
sweatshirt (for hat) or knit hat ✦ Green sweatpants

1 Lay dessert plate on fabric and trace around it with
chalk. Repeat until you have 5 circles in each shade of
fabric. Cut out all 10 circles.

2 Sew around circumference of each fabric circle, about
½" from edge, using a running stitch. When circle is
complete, pull thread to gather fabric, tucking in raw
edge as you gather. Fill pouch with fiberfill until round
and taut. Sew opening closed. Repeat for each circle.

3 Loosely stitch grapes together in desired formation,
then sew cluster to sweatshirt.

4 Using copier, create large and small leaf templates as
desired. Cut out shapes. Use chalk to trace 9 small
and 6 large leaves on green felt; cut out. Use green
marker to draw leaf veins. Reserve 3 small leaves for hat.
Glue leaves together in groups of 2 or 3, then stitch or
glue leaf groups onto grape cluster, as desired.

5 If using sweatshirt for hat, cut off 1 sleeve and follow
step 3 for tomato costume (left). If using knit hat,
sew felt leaves to top of hat.

Cute & creepy

The costumes here make use of repurposed items, like gloves (for a spider) and an umbrella (for bat wings).

Butterfly

⋙☠⋘

YOU'LL NEED ✦ **Monarch butterfly kite ($23; kiteandwind.com)** ✦ **Scissors** ✦ **Yellow sweatshirt** ✦ **Safety pins** ✦ **Needle and thread** ✦ **2 large, round orange beads** ✦ **2 black pipe cleaners** ✦ **Hot-glue gun** ✦ **Black headband** ✦ **Black leggings**

1 Cut kite in half, down center. Lay sweatshirt flat, face up. Arrange each half of kite along side seam of shirt body and sleeves; pin each one in place. Stitch wings to sweatshirt.

2 Thread one bead onto each pipe cleaner. Secure with glue. Twist pipe cleaners around headband and glue.

Spider

YOU'LL NEED ✦ **Needle and thread**
✦ **½ yard black fabric** ✦ **Cotton balls**
✦ **3 pairs black gloves** ✦ **Safety pins,**
optional ✦ **Black sweat suit with hood**
✦ **Black yarn or string** ✦ **Black sneakers**
✦ **Purple face makeup** ✦ **Black lipstick**

1 Sew 2 tubes, each about length of child's arm span, out of black fabric. Fill with cotton.

2 Attach 1 pair of gloves to ends of both tubes; sew or safety-pin tubes to back of sweatshirt. Use yarn or string to attach arms to each other and to sleeves of sweatshirt (so all arms move together). Put sweat suit, sneakers and last pair of gloves on child.

3 Apply face makeup and lipstick and pull up hood.

MONKEY

YOU'LL NEED ✦ Scissors ✦ 1 sheet each of pink and brown felt ✦ Needle and thread ✦ Fabric glue, safety pins; optional ✦ Brown sweat suit with hood ✦ ¼ yard brown fabric ✦ Cotton balls ✦ 1 pair large cream-color gloves

1 Cut shapes for monkey ears from brown felt. Then cut slightly smaller ear overlays from pink felt. Sew or glue pink felt to brown felt. Sew ears to sweatshirt hood or attach with safety pins.

2 Pin brown fabric into a tube to form a narrow tail; sew. Stuff tail with cotton balls. Sew or safety-pin tail to seat of sweat suit. Put gloves on feet.

Prized pig

❧ ☠ ❧

YOU'LL NEED ✦ **Scissors** ✦ **Needle and thread** ✦ **Fabric glue** ✦ **Safety pins, optional** ✦ **1 sheet each of white, pink and black felt** ✦ **White sweat suit with hood** ✦ **¼ yard pink stretch material** ✦ **Cotton balls** ✦ **1 pipe cleaner** ✦ **Gold cardboard** ✦ **Sticker reading** NUMBER 1 ✦ **Hole punch** ✦ **Key ring** ✦ **2 yards brown ribbon** ✦ **Card stock** ✦ **Thin white elastic** ✦ **1 pair white socks** ✦ **White sneakers**

1 Cut ears from white felt. Cut slightly smaller ear overlays from pink felt. Sew or glue pink felt to white. Sew or safety-pin ears to hood.

2 Pin pink fabric into a tube for tail; sew. Stuff with cotton balls. Insert pipe cleaner and twist tube into spiral. Sew or safety-pin to seat of sweat suit.

3 Cut medal out of gold cardboard and affix NUMBER 1 sticker. Punch a hole in top of medal and insert key ring. Thread ribbon through key ring and tie around child's neck.

4 Glue white felt to card stock. Cut out nose pieces: a circle and a rectangle. Roll rectangle into a tube and glue edges together; glue circle to 1 end of tube. Cut nostrils from black felt; glue to nose.

5 Punch 1 hole in each side of nose. Run elastic through holes and tie it behind head. Put socks on hands; put on sneakers.

Flower girl

✎❧☙✍

YOU'LL NEED ✦ **2 yellow wristbands** ✦ **Tape measure** ✦ **Scissors** ✦ **1 20" x 30" sheet pink poster board** ✦ **1 yard yellow felt** ✦ **Hot-glue gun** ✦ **Petal templates (pages 185–186)** ✦ **Pencil** ✦ **Self-adhesive Velcro fasteners** ✦ **Paper clip** ✦ **Yellow leotard** ✦ **Green tights** ✦ **Pink shoes**

1 Measure child's waist and head, and add 2" to both measurements. Using these lengths, cut a 2"-wide waistband for tutu and a 1¼"-wide headband for crown out of pink poster board. Cut a 1½"-wide band for tutu and ¾"-wide band for crown out of yellow felt.

2 Center felt waistband and headband on respective poster-board bands and adhere with hot glue.

3 Cut out templates, making sure to include tab at bottom of each petal. Trace around templates on felt and poster board with pencil, then cut. Make 8 large petals and 22 small ones out of pink poster board, plus 8 large-petal overlays and 22 small-petal overlays out of yellow felt.

4 Glue yellow felt overlays to poster-board cutouts to make petals.

5 Lay tutu waistband on table, yellow-felt side down. Overlap large petals evenly; tabs should be 2" to 3" apart when yellow-felt side is up. Glue tabs to waistband.

6 Wrap waistband around child, and mark where it will fasten. Adhere Velcro strips to the proper places.

7 Lay crown headband on table, felt side down. Overlap 10 small petals evenly, felt side up. Glue tabs to headband.

8 Glue ends of headband together to fit child's head. Secure with paper clip until dry, then remove clip.

9 Glue 6 small petals to inside of each wristband. Let dry.

10 Once costume is on, bend petals into desired position.

USE AN UMBRELLA TO MAKE THESE WINGS.

Scary bat

৩❀৩

YOU'LL NEED ✦ Scissors ✦ Bat ear and fang templates (page 187) ✦ 3 9" x 12" pieces of felt: 1 pink, 1 black, 1 white ✦ Pencil ✦ Black baseball cap ✦ Hot-glue gun ✦ Pair of extra-large googly eyes (available at crafts stores) ✦ Large black nylon umbrella ✦ Safety pins, optional ✦ Dark gray thermal or fleece top and pants ✦ Black sneakers ✦ Black socks ✦ Black gloves

1 Cut out and trace templates to make 2 ears from black felt, 2 ear overlays from pink felt and 4 fangs from white felt. Cut out all shapes.

2 Center each overlay on an ear and glue. Cut 2 slits on top of baseball cap in front of seams at 10 o'clock and 2 o'clock. Slip ear tabs through slits so that pink overlays face cap's bill. Glue tabs to inside of cap. Tilt ears forward and shape.

3 Mark each fang with a dotted line as shown on template. Glue each pair together, from point to dotted line.

4 Apply hot glue to tabs on fangs and attach tabs to underside of cap's bill. Glue googly eyes to front of cap.

5 Separate umbrella fabric from metal skeleton, leaving metal tips intact. Cut fabric in half to form a semicircle. With pins or glue, attach semicircle to shoulders and along sleeves of thermal top. Work from underneath so that when you flip circle into place, pins or glue are hidden.

Once upon a time

Create fantastical characters who might have stepped out of a fairy tale. On this night a neighborhood becomes a kingdom!

Pretty princess

YOU'LL NEED ✦ Pencil ✦ Scissors ✦ Child's long dress ✦ Iridescent fabric, 2 to 4 yards depending on child's size ✦ Blue lace, 2 to 4 yards depending on child's size ✦ White tights ✦ Silver shoes ✦ Silver cord, 3 times size of child's waist) ✦ Silver and white ribbon, 2 yards each ✦ White fake fur ✦ Wand (from costume or toy store) ✦ Silver cardboard ✦ Glue ✦ Gems and glitter ✦ Hole punch ✦ White elastic ✦ Silvery lipstick

1 Trace shape of child's long dress on iridescent fabric. Cut front and back, and sew together to make sleeveless bottom layer of costume dress.

2 Trace shape of child's long dress on lace. Cut out into front, back and sleeves for top layer. Sew back and front of overdress together. Sew sleeves and attach sleeves to bodice. Trim neckline with scissors.

3 Have child put on dress, tights and shoes. Wrap silver cord around waist 3 times and tie into a bow. Tie ribbons around upper arms and blouse fabric to give sleeves puffy effect.

4 Cut white fake fur to create a stole. Make slits in sides of stole; thread white ribbon through slits to make arm loops. Tie more ribbon around wand as desired.

5 Cut crown out of silver cardboard; glue or staple it together in back. Glue gems and glitter to it. Punch holes in sides of crown and thread elastic through them for chin strap. Apply lipstick.

NOBLE KNIGHT

YOU'LL NEED ✦ Red fabric, 1 to 2 yards depending on child's size ✦ Scissors ✦ Gray sweat suit with hood ✦ Brown boots ✦ Gold fabric, ½ yard ✦ Glue ✦ Wide gold ribbon, 2 yards ✦ Metallic cardboard sheets, 1 silver, 1 white, 1 red ✦ Narrow red ribbon ✦ 2 yards red Velcro ✦ Toy sword (plastic)

1 Fold red fabric in half and cut out hole for head, forming back and front of tunic. Dress child in sweat suit and boots.

2 Cut lion emblem (find on Internet) from gold fabric and glue to front of tunic. Glue gold ribbon along bottom of tunic for trim. Pull hood of sweat suit through tunic's neckline. Tie remaining gold ribbon at waist for belt.

3 Cut shield out of white cardboard. Cut 2 slits on each side of shield; thread red ribbon through slits, then tie to form 2 loops big enough for arm to fit through. Trace shield shape onto silver cardboard and cut out; glue pieces together. Cut lion emblem out of red cardboard; glue to shield. Slide shield over child's arm, through ribbon loops.

4 Cut silver cardboard to form armor of arm and shin guards. Glue Velcro along edges of arm and shin guards. Attach arm guards, pulling out sweatshirt cuffs. Attach leg guards to child's legs, forming cuffs with sweat suit over boots.

Flying Broom Spell

Mix together magic dust and bee wings Wave a broom above your head and say -- Hocus-Pocus.

Spook Spell

You Need:
1 Black Cat
2 Sprinkles of Ghostly Horror
3 Loud Screams
Mix Well

Abracadabra!

Embrace the magical side of Halloween with these witchy costumes. Use your newfound powers to cast a spell ensuring a fun time for all.

Spider witch

ೋ❦ೋ

YOU'LL NEED ✦ **Sheer black fabric, 1 yard** ✦ **Measuring tape** ✦ **Pinking shears** ✦ **½"-wide black ribbon, 1 yard** ✦ **Large and small plastic spiders** ✦ **Hot-glue gun** ✦ **Scissors** ✦ **"Fun fur" or "eyelash" yarn** ✦ **Velcro tabs** ✦ **Black leotard** ✦ **Spider webbing** ✦ **Stiffened felt (available at craft stores), 1 sheet** ✦ **Black tights**

1 Make skirt: Lay sheer fabric on a flat surface. Measure child's waist; double that measurement, then cut fabric to this length. Cut a jagged bottom edge with pinking shears.

2 Cut ½" slits, 1" apart and 1" from top edge of fabric, along its full length. Weave ribbon through slits.

3 Using hot-glue gun, attach a large spider to front of skirt. Cut 3" to 4" lengths of yarn. Glue 1 end of each to inside jagged edge of skirt and glue a small spider to other end.

4 Make sleeves: Measure from child's shoulder to elbow and add 3". Cut 2 pieces of sheer fabric this length (should be comfortable and safe) and 12" wide. Cut a jagged bottom edge with pinking shears.

5 Glue sheer fabric to armhole seam by placing ½" dabs of glue 1" apart. Start at armpit and work around sleeve. Gather fabric between spots of glue so material will not detach when sleeve stretches. Repeat on other arm.

6 Hang spiders from jagged edges. Glue webbing and spiders to front of leotard.

7 Make headpiece: Cut a pointed shape out of felt; glue on spiders.

8 Glue Velcro on bottom ½" of headpiece and back of leotard collar (outside). Attach pieces.

Flying Broom Spell
Mix together magic dust and bee wings. Wave a broom above your head and say -- Hocus Pocus.

Spookie Spell
You Need:
1 Black Cat
2 Sprinkles of Ghostly Horror
3 Loud Screams
Mix Well

CALL ON YOUR IMAGINATION TO CONJURE MAGIC INCANTATIONS.

Book of spells

YOU'LL NEED ✦ Measuring tape ✦ Scissors ✦ 2 yards white felt ✦ Hot-glue gun ✦ Wide, single-fold gold bias tape ✦ Black marker ✦ Glitter glue ✦ Plastic lizards ✦ Stick-on Velcro strips ✦ White long-sleeve T-shirt ✦ White leggings

1 Have your child stand with arms stretched out to sides. Measure from wrist to wrist across child's back, then from shoulder blades to top of thigh. Cut white felt to these measurements.

2 Lay felt flat. At each end of "book," glue gold bias tape along felt edge. Affix a second layer of bias tape slightly overlapping the first, and a third slightly overlapping the second. Measure 6" from top of book and write your spells with black marker. Use glitter glue to color and embellish their titles; let glue dry overnight. Stick plastic lizards wherever you desire on book.

3 Affix 1 side of Velcro strip along top edge of book. Stick 1" pieces of other side of Velcro strip to back of leotard arms. Have child put on shirt and leggings. Attach book to child's back using Velcro.

Bubbling cauldron

❧☠❧

YOU'LL NEED ✦ Measuring tape ✦ Scissors ✦ Cardboard ✦ Hot-glue gun ✦ Serrated knife ✦ 1 yard blue fabric (to resemble water) ✦ 1½ yards black felt ✦ ¼ yard orange felt ✦ Yellow felt square ✦ Red felt square ✦ Needle, black thread ✦ ½"-wide elastic, 1 yard ✦ Safety pin ✦ Plastic frogs, lizards, bones, eyeballs ✦ 1"- and 1½"-diameter Styrofoam balls ✦ Poly-Fil ✦ Newspaper or tissue paper ✦ Black shirt ✦ Black pants

1 Measure child's head; add 2". Cut a circular hole of this diameter from cardboard. Measure 7" to 8" out from edge of hole; cut outside circle to form a ring. Glue blue fabric to front of ring. Trim fabric; leave 3" overhang all around. Glue edges to back. Trim hole; leave 2" to 3" of extra fabric. Cut slits in fabric overhang; glue to back.

2 Measure perimeter of ring; add 3" and note measurement. Cut 4 (24" long) oval pieces (determine width by dividing noted number by 4) from black felt. Make sure widest part of oval is double width of edges.

3 Lay out 1 felt oval. Run glue along edge of longer side. Place second oval on top of first; press glued seam together; let dry. Open ovals with seam facing down. Run glue down free edge of one attached oval. Place another oval on top of it; glue as above. Repeat process with last oval. Close cauldron tube by gluing together outer ovals' edges. Turn cauldron right-side out. Cut orange, red and yellow felt into flame shapes. Glue to cauldron. Turn cauldron inside out. Stitch 1" pocket on bottom edge; leave 1" opening for access. Thread elastic through and join ends with safety pin. Turn cauldron right side out. Glue ring to top of cauldron by folding 1" of felt over top edge and adhering. Cut armholes 3" to 4" from top of cauldron. Glue animals, bones, eyeballs, foam balls and Poly-Fil to "water."

4 Place cauldron over child's head, with arms through side holes. Adjust elastic on bottom so it is snug around child's legs. Stuff with newspaper or tissue paper.

GET CREATIVE
The more things you add to the top, the better! Consider rubber snakes, a bone-shaped dog treat and even the arm and leg of a doll. If you add more Poly-Fil, the concoction will look steamier.

Templates

Here you'll find the templates mentioned in some of the craft instructions. To use one, reproduce it on a copy machine or scan it into a computer and print out. Reduce, enlarge or use at 100 percent, as per directions on the page.

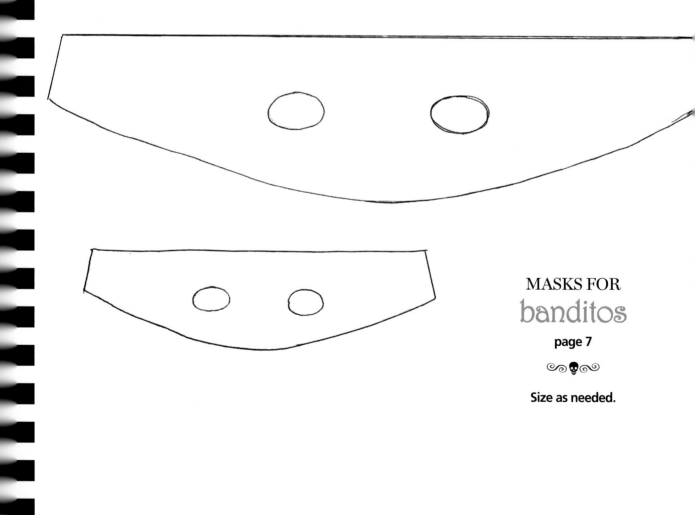

MASKS FOR

banditos

page 7

Size as needed.

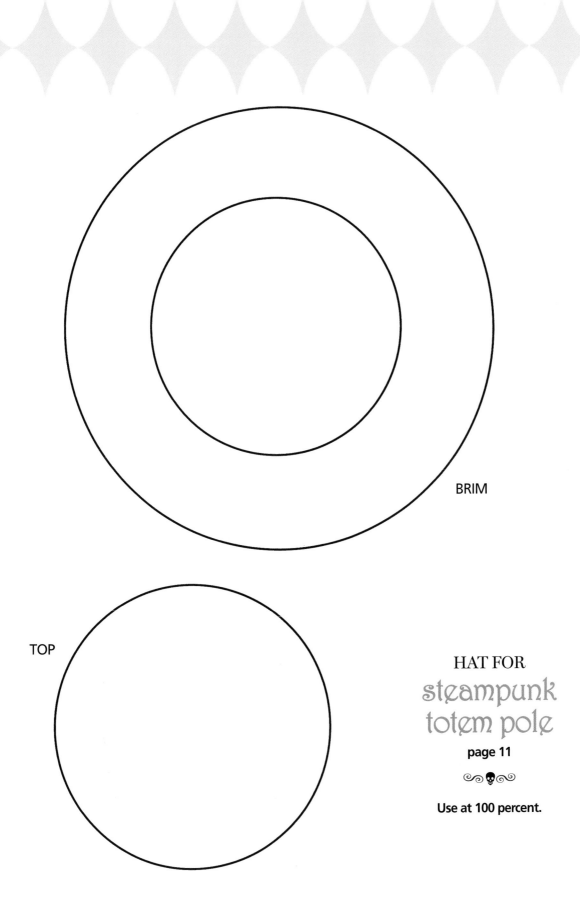

BRIM

TOP

HAT FOR
steampunk
totem pole
page 11

Use at 100 percent.

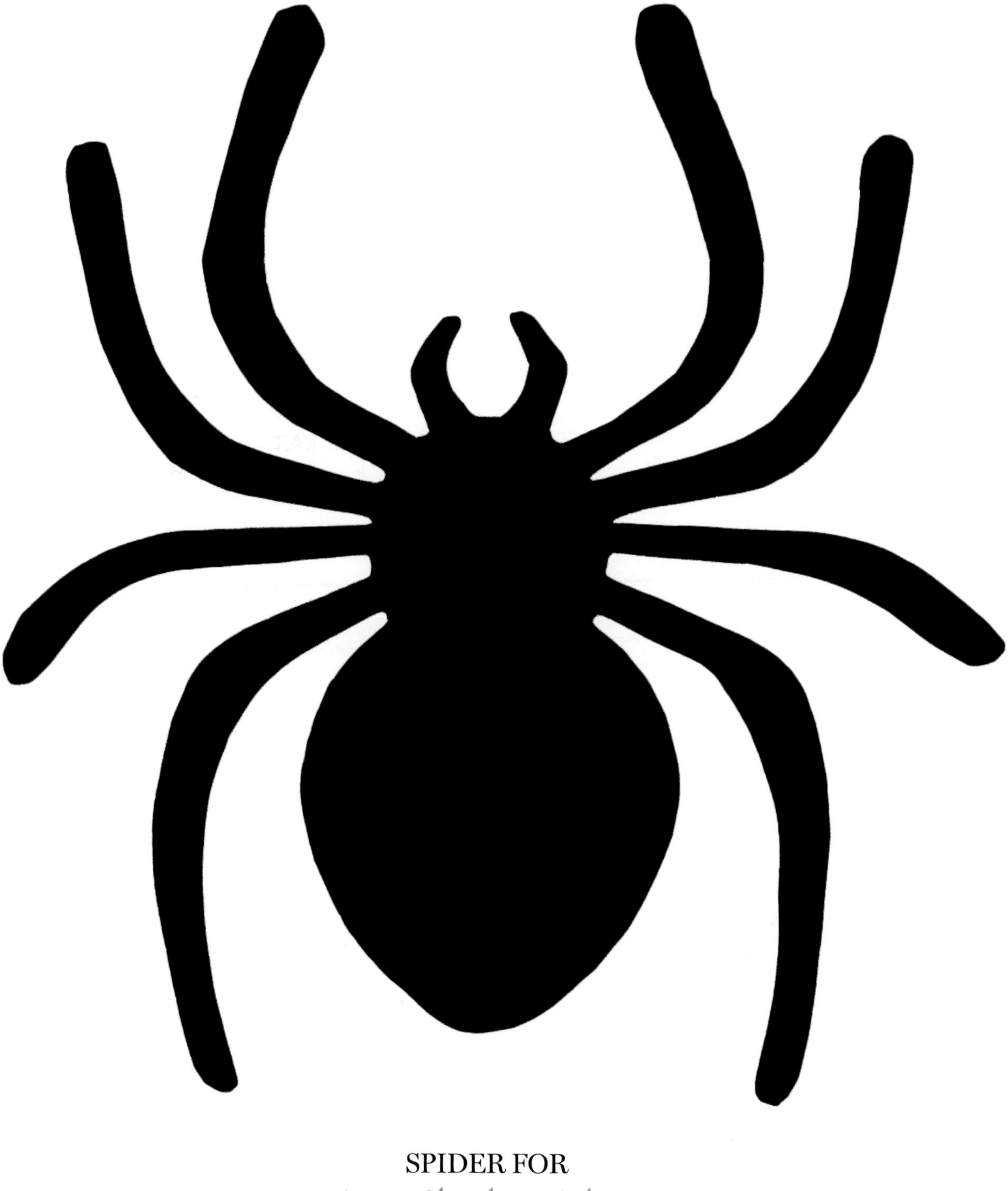

SPIDER FOR
stenciled spiders
AND creepy lanterns
page 13, stenciled spiders; page 47, creepy lanterns

Size as needed.

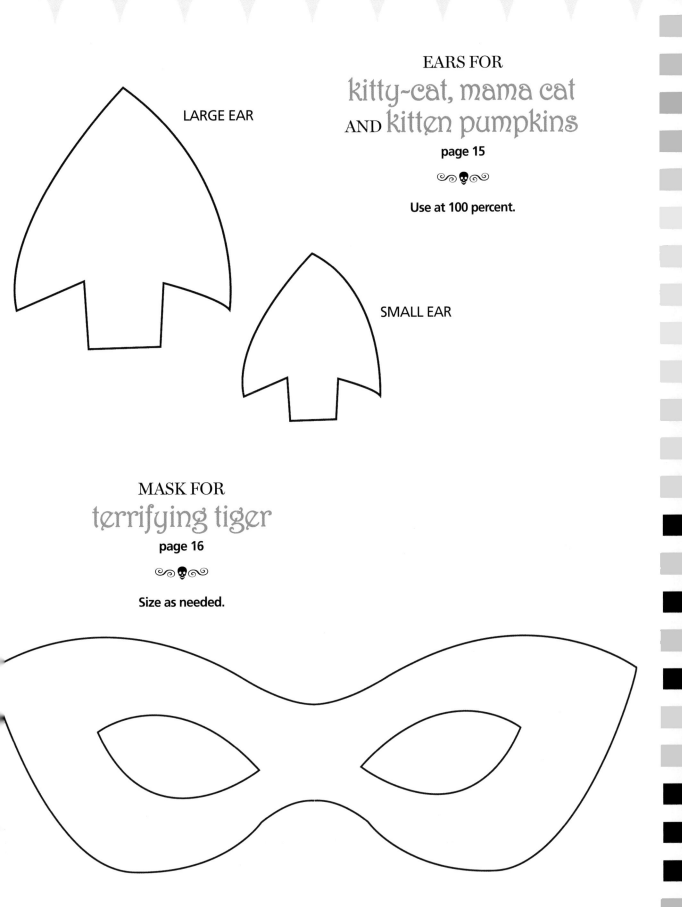

LARGE EAR

EARS FOR
kitty~cat, mama cat
AND kitten pumpkins
page 15

Use at 100 percent.

SMALL EAR

MASK FOR
terrifying tiger
page 16

Size as needed.

HAT BRIM AND CONE FOR
nosy faces, friendly witch
AND witchy candy jars

page 19, nosy faces and friendly witch; page 53, witchy candy jars

☙ 💀 ☜

Size as needed.

BRIM

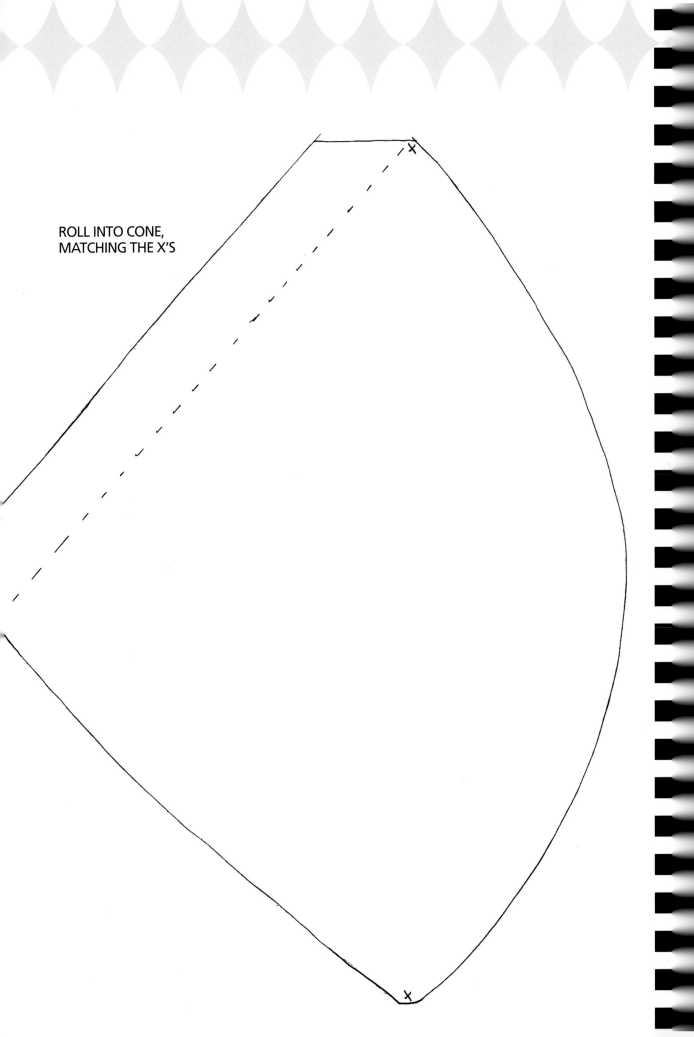

ROLL INTO CONE,
MATCHING THE X'S

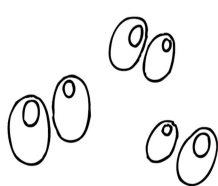

EYES FOR
furry door
page 24

☙ ☠ ☙

Size as needed.

EYE FOR
screaming door face
page 26

ᘒᖇ ☠ ᖇᘒ

Use at 100 percent.

SMALL BAT FOR
bat storm AND clip-on bats
page 30, bat storm; page 53, clip-on bats

For bat storm: Size as needed.
For clip-on bats: Use at 100 percent.

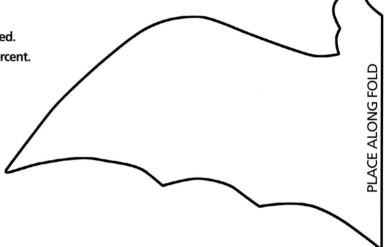

PLACE ALONG FOLD

LARGE BAT FOR
bat storm
page 30

Size as needed.

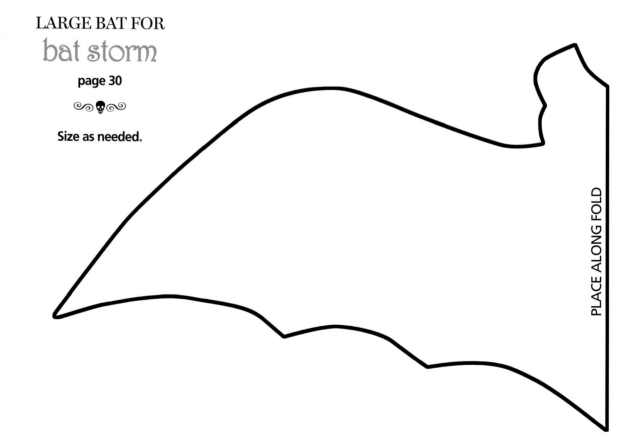

PLACE ALONG FOLD

WITCH AND MOON FOR
witchy luminarias

page 36

⤳ ☠ ⤳

Use at 100 percent.

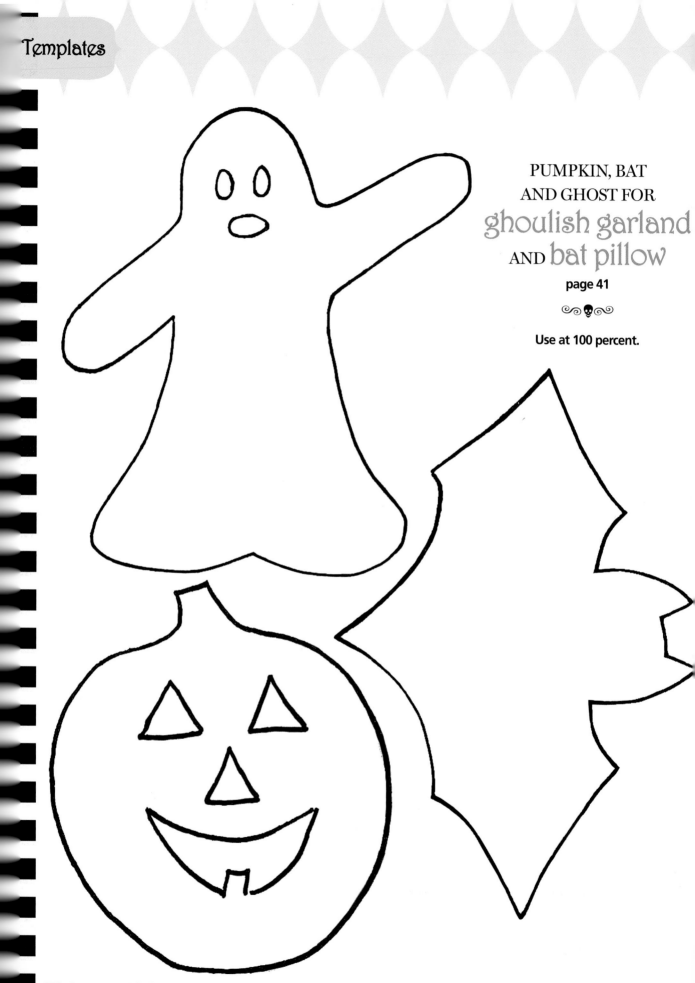

PUMPKIN, BAT
AND GHOST FOR
ghoulish garland
AND bat pillow

page 41

Use at 100 percent.

PUMPKIN, BAT AND GHOST FOR
tin-can lantern
AND Halloween mobile

page 42, tin-can lantern; page 49, Halloween mobile

Use at 100 percent.

TREE FOR
spooky trees
page 50

☙ ☠ ❧

Use at 100 percent.

LEAVES FOR
leaf elbow patches
AND leaf garland

page 60, leaf elbow patches; page 61, leaf garland

☙ ☠ ❧

Use at 100 percent.

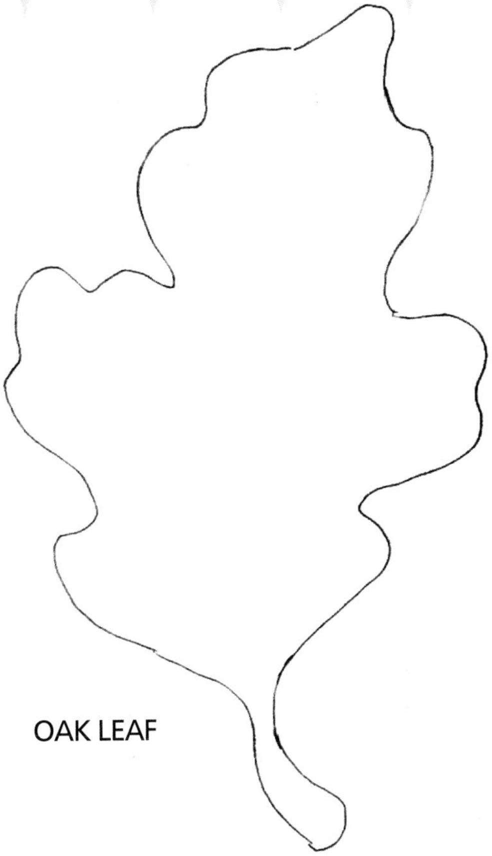

OAK LEAF

MAPLE LEAF

SPIDER FOR
spider napkin rings

page 66

☙ ☠ ❧

Use at 100 percent.

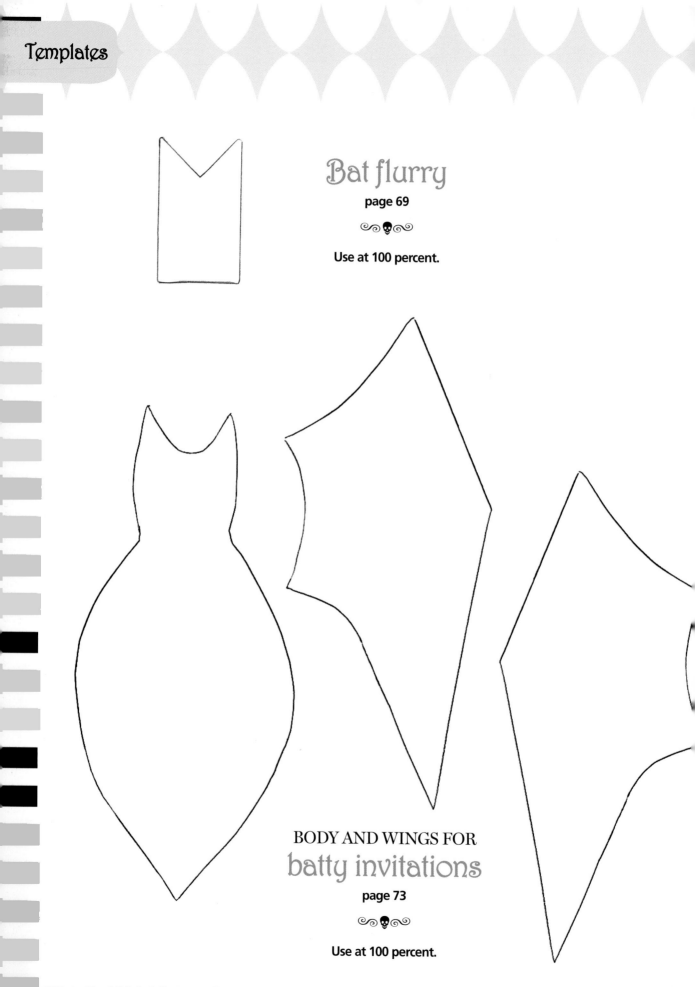

Bat flurry

page 69

Use at 100 percent.

BODY AND WINGS FOR

batty invitations

page 73

Use at 100 percent.

Bat mobile

page 77

Size as needed.

SPIKES FOR
little lizard
page 138

Use at 100 percent.

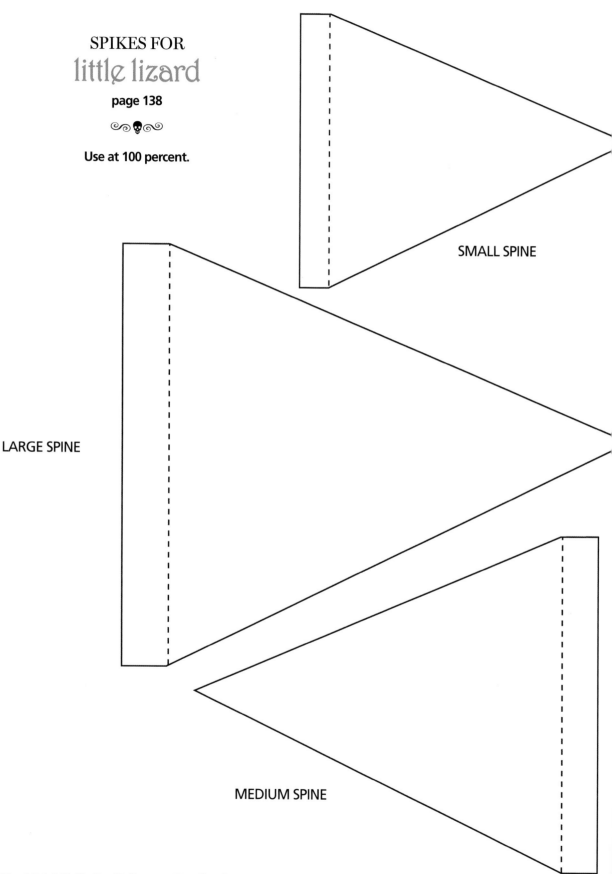

SMALL SPINE

LARGE SPINE

MEDIUM SPINE

CAT FOR
goody bag
page 143

Use at 100 percent.

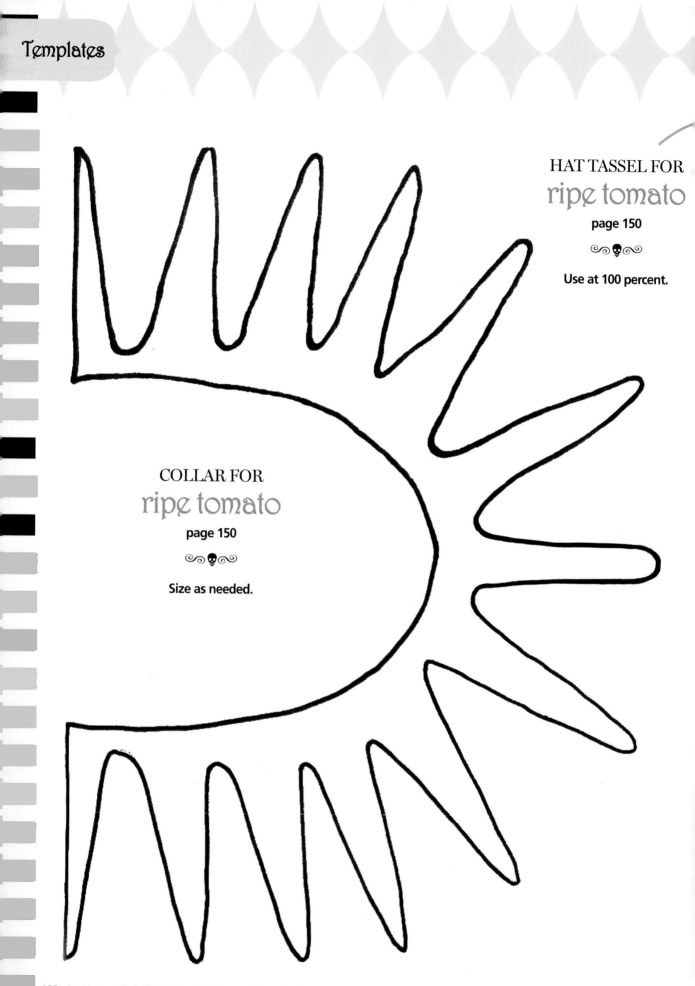

HAT TASSEL FOR
ripe tomato
page 150
෩ ☠ ෨
Use at 100 percent.

COLLAR FOR
ripe tomato
page 150
෩ ☠ ෨
Size as needed.

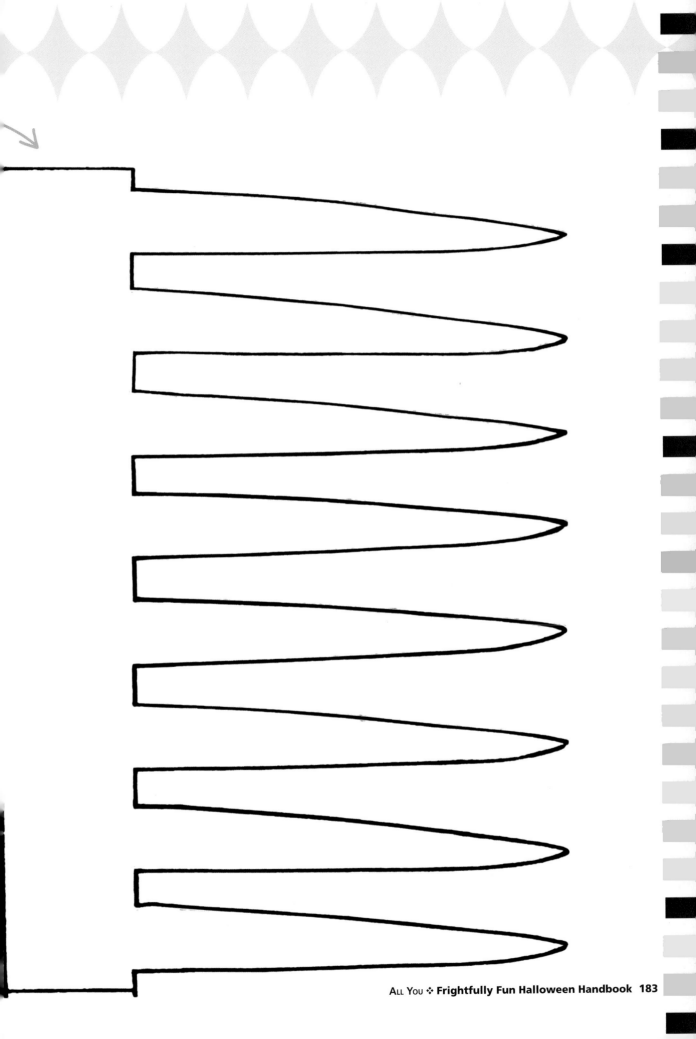

LEAF FOR
bunch of grapes
page 151

Size as needed.

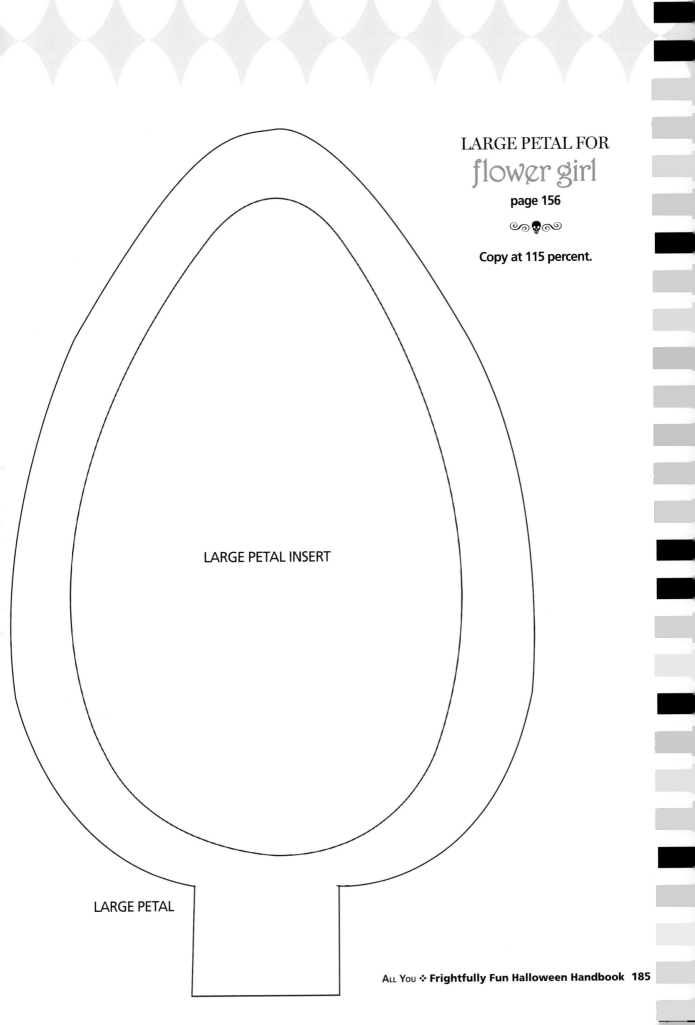

LARGE PETAL FOR
flower girl
page 156

Copy at 115 percent.

LARGE PETAL INSERT

LARGE PETAL

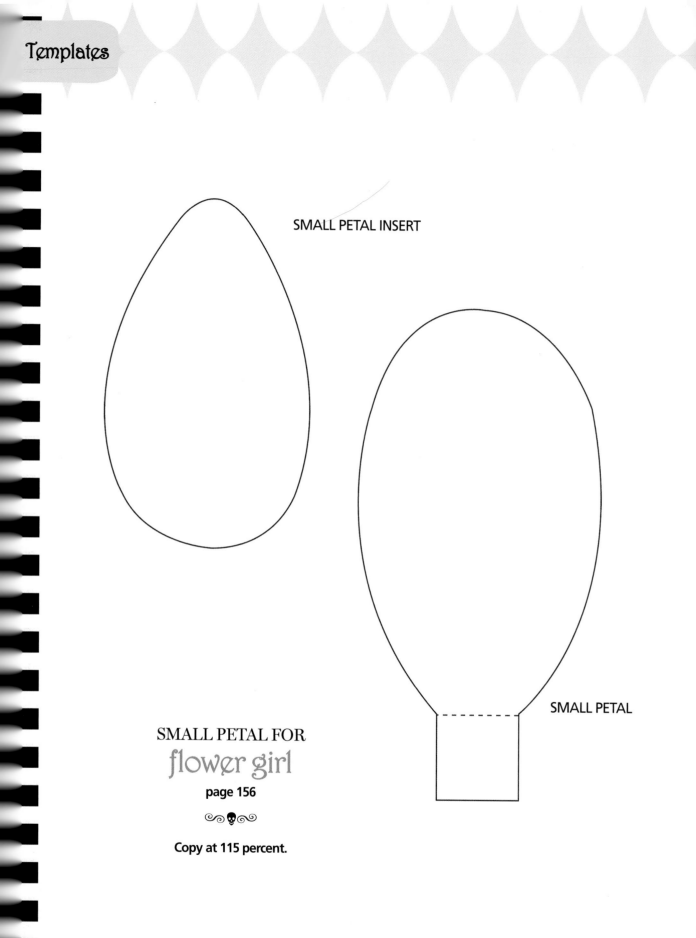

SMALL PETAL INSERT

SMALL PETAL

SMALL PETAL FOR

flower girl

page 156

Copy at 115 percent.

EAR AND FANG FOR
scary bat
page 157

෬ඹ෬

Use at 100 percent.

BAT EAR INSERT

BAT FANG

BAT EAR

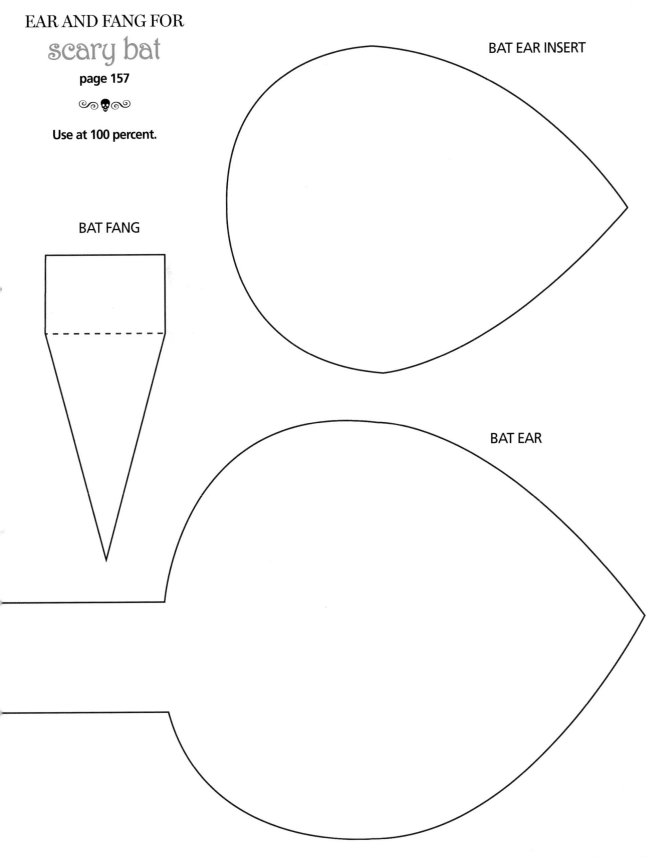

Index

Costumes

Templates

Get to know All You

EVERY ISSUE OF ALL YOU MAGAZINE shows busy readers how to whip up creative decorations and projects, organize fun get-togethers and make delicious meals and treats. Our recipes and crafts are always affordable, with easy-to-follow instructions that don't require a huge investment of time. In this exciting Halloween guide, ALL YOU editors have gathered their favorite seasonal recipes, crafts and party ideas so you can celebrate in eerie splendor with minimal hassle.

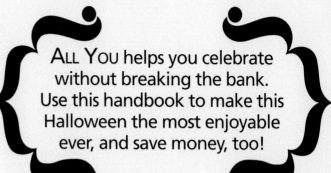

ALL YOU helps you celebrate without breaking the bank. Use this handbook to make this Halloween the most enjoyable ever, and save money, too!

ALL YOU, published monthly by Time Inc., helps women enjoy life for less. The magazine includes coupons and strategies for saving money; budget-friendly, easy-to-prepare recipes; fashion for real body types; cleaning and organizing ideas; craft projects; diet and exercise advice that fits a busy lifestyle; practical beauty tips; inspirational stories; and much more. ALL YOU is available by subscription and at Walmart stores nationwide as well as other select outlets. Visit allyou.com.

Credits

OUR THANKS TO EVERYONE WHO CONTRIBUTED TO THIS BOOK, INCLUDING:

Photographers
Antonis Achilleos
Ryan Benyi
Margaret Gibbons
Aimee Herring
Scott Jones
Sean Knox
Barbara Peacock
Don Penny
Charles Schiller
Kate Sears
Mark Thomas

Prop stylists
Elizabeth Blake
Dwyer Paulsen
Davida Sidrane
Linda Whyte
Gerri Williams

Food stylists
A.J. Battifarano
Tara Bench
Paul Grimes
Lynn Miller
Joyce Sangirardi
Karen Tack
Susan Vajaranant

Craft stylists
Sarah Cave
Bella Foster
Lori Hellender
Ingrid Leess
Jayna Maleri
Lisa McGee
Matthew Mead
Jean Nayer
David Verruni

Resources

SHOP ONLINE FOR GREAT PRICES AND HARD-TO-FIND ITEMS

candywarehouse.com Offers a selection of current and nostalgic brands. Allows you to shop for candy by color.

createforless.com Good prices on all sorts of craft supplies.

funkins.com Purveyor of carveable faux pumpkins—great for craft projects that you want to save and reuse.

grandinroad.com An interesting assortment of indoor and outdoor Halloween decorations (in season only).

100candles.com One-stop shopping for candles of different sizes and colors, at affordable prices.

orientaltrading.com Wide array of party and craft supplies at reasonable prices.

ribbonbazaar.com One-stop shopping for ribbon and trim.

save-on-crafts.com Party and decorating items, plus craft supplies.

suncatchereyes.com An assortment of eyes that are typically used for stuffed animals, used in this book for some of the cat pumpkins.